KS2 SATs Practice Papers

30 English Spelling Tests for Year 6

New Edition Updated for 2020

With FREE ADDITIONAL CONTENT Online

Ages 10-11

About this Book

This book contains **30 complete, fully up-to-date** Spelling Practice Tests for Year 6 students.

Closely modelled on the **most recent** SATs Paper 2 exams, these tests assess 600 age-appropriate words, including **all 100 words** in the **government's word list for Years 5 & 6**.

Like the actual exam, each Test consists of **20 questions** that assess the student's **spelling**, with each correct answer being worth 1 mark.

Also included in this book are:
- The complete, realistic **exam-style Test Transcripts** for all thirty Tests.
- Full, easy-to-follow **instructions for adults on how to administer** the tests and **marking guidelines**.
- **Complete Spelling Lists** for each of the tests.
- Useful **Instructions for Students** that provide a straightforward explanation of what to expect in a spelling test.

For quick reference, at the bottom of the page of each Practice Test, you will find the page number of the corresponding Test Transcript.

Get your
FREE
ADDITIONAL CONTENT ONLINE
with this QR code:

(includes a printable HOW WELL I DID pamphlet & STUDENT 10-MINUTE TEST DIARY)

Want even more? Then why not explore our growing collection of
FREE PRINTABLE
EDUTAINMENT & EDUCATIONAL RESOURCES?
Find them here:

(includes printable worksheets, word lists & word games)

Alternatively, you can get your
Free Additional Content Online for this book @ **http://bit.ly/STPBooks2JhvoHL**
Free Edutainment & Educational Resources @ **www.swottotspublishing.com/free-from-stp-books**

Published by STP Books
An imprint of Swot Tots Publishing Ltd
Kemp House
152-160 City Road
London EC1V 2NX

www.swottotspublishing.com

Text, design, and layout © Swot Tots Publishing Ltd

First published 2017 by Swot Tots Publishing Ltd
This edition published 2019 by STP Books

STP Books have asserted their moral right under the Copyright, Designs and Patents Act, 1988, to be identified as the author of this work.

Typeset, cover design, and inside concept design by Swot Tots Publishing Ltd.

British Library Cataloguing in Publication Data. A catalogue record for this book is available from the British Library.

ISBN 978-1-912956-06-7

Contents

INSTRUCTIONS FOR STUDENTS

PLEASE READ THE FOLLOWING INSTRUCTIONS <u>CAREFULLY</u> BEFORE PROCEEDING WITH ANY OF THE PRACTICE TEST PAPERS IN THIS BOOK.

Doing the Spelling Tests

In each Practice Test Paper in this book, your **spelling** will be tested.

Each Test is made up of **20 sentences**. All of these sentences appear in your book.

In each sentence, a word has been left out and **a blank space** has been provided for you **to write the correctly spelt word**.

Your Test Administrator will read each missing word out to you **FOUR times** in total.

To begin with, you will hear the word **three times** close together:
- The Administrator will say the word once on its own;
- Then read the word in its given sentence;
- And then say the word on its own once more.

Listen carefully and then **write** the **correctly spelt word** in the **blank space**.

After the Administrator has done this for each sentence, you will hear each of the missing words for **the fourth and last time** when the Administrator reads all 20 sentences out again from the beginning.

Time

Every test should take about **15 minutes** – however, your Test Administrator will give you as much time as you need.

Good luck!

1   This book falls into the _____ of historical fiction.   1 mark

2   We all _____ the seriousness of the situation.   1 mark

3   The man who lives upstairs is an odd _____.   1 mark

4   _____ are found in almost all natural habitats.   1 mark

5   Recycling is clearly good for the _____.   1 mark

6   The wealthy merchant was forced to _____ his will.   1 mark

7   "I've got a massive _____ on my arm," whined Ian.   1 mark

8   "That is utterly _____!" scoffed Ravi.   1 mark

9   Being able to speak a second _____ can be very useful.   1 mark

10   Nadine's father is a famous civil _____.   1 mark

11   "Might I _____ the onion soup, sir?" said the waiter.   1 mark

12   There is a _____ change in Polly's attitude.   1 mark

13   "I'm too old for a _____!" complained Jan.   1 mark

14   Vera cried at the _____ of being wrongly blamed.   1 mark

15   "That lady looks _____," mused Kate.   1 mark

16   The twins' story was terrible as it was so _____.   1 mark

17   The crooked lawyer _____ many of his clients.   1 mark

18   The hotel is happy to _____ guests with pets.   1 mark

19   That government wasn't _____ elected.   1 mark

20   The most hard-working _____ is the heart.   1 mark

1   The pirates hid their stolen _____ in a Cornish cave.   1 mark

2   "_____ responsible for this mess?" demanded the cook.   1 mark

3   That _____ never gives new writers good reviews.   1 mark

4   Tina loved her grandmother's _____ stew.   1 mark

5   The fairy made the knight's knapsack _____ vanish.   1 mark

6   You need a _____ screwdriver for that.   1 mark

7   I have no _____ that our team will win their match.   1 mark

8   Last _____, Jeff didn't go to work because he was ill.   1 mark

9   Our local community will _____ from these changes.   1 mark

10   Parking is not _____ in this area.   1 mark

11   Will is being punished because he _____ at school.   1 mark

12   _____ for Helena, we all went on the class trip.   1 mark

13   Margaret is a very _____ driver.   1 mark

14   Many people have a bowl of _____ for breakfast.   1 mark

15   Lulu works for a _____ shop in Devon.   1 mark

16   The customer complained that her steak was too _____.   1 mark

17   The teacher lined the students up in order of _____.   1 mark

18   "Your fingernails are a _____," grumbled Tom's mother.   1 mark

19   Tragically, this disaster was _____.   1 mark

20   The assumption that Shakespeare wrote this is _____.   1 mark

Test Administrator Transcript 2 on page 36

1 The _____ has promised to look into this matter. 1 mark

2 The children found the _____ a bit dull. 1 mark

3 The _____ used to be a very popular dance. 1 mark

4 "A cup of hot cocoa sounds positively _____!" said Val. 1 mark

5 I find Latin _____ rather confusing. 1 mark

6 Alan feels that Josh _____ the situation. 1 mark

7 Rita has bought a new _____ for her garden. 1 mark

8 The word _____ is misused all the time. 1 mark

9 Some people think London needs a new _____ airport. 1 mark

10 "Drink this; it will help _____ the pain," said the nurse. 1 mark

11 Lemon juice can be used as a kind of _____ ink. 1 mark

12 The _____ events that followed stunned everyone. 1 mark

13 My favourite part of that song is the _____. 1 mark

14 _____ option 2 if you do not wish us to email you. 1 mark

15 Could you _____ these oranges, please? 1 mark

16 Clara's new kitten is _____ cute. 1 mark

17 I dislike _____, but I love sardines. 1 mark

18 My aunt was very _____ when she was in her twenties. 1 mark

19 Molly is taking a Spanish _____. 1 mark

20 "I think you'd look nice in that _____ jacket," said Jim. 1 mark

1   A group of owls is called a _____ of owls.   1 mark

2   The headmaster shook his head slowly in _____.   1 mark

3   Please _____ your receipt of this email.   1 mark

4   An _____ silence settled over the audience.   1 mark

5   Hugo gets very _____ when he is hungry.   1 mark

6   I can't _____ apple juice; it makes me feel sick.   1 mark

7   La Traviata is the most expensive _____ in Milan.   1 mark

8   A magpie landed on the uppermost _____ of the tree.   1 mark

9   Next Monday, the _____ will meet to discuss this.   1 mark

10   "I've made my _____," declared Rufus stubbornly.   1 mark

11   A wide _____ of fresh fruit was on sale in the canteen.   1 mark

12   You will need two _____ of milk to make the sauce.   1 mark

13   Disa gave no _____ for her week-long absence.   1 mark

14   Ted _____ a recent photograph to the form.   1 mark

15   Even though these sandals look _____, they aren't.   1 mark

16   "Don't _____," snapped Jorge. "I know what to do."   1 mark

17   I found the _____ in that book rather irritating.   1 mark

18   "What would you be willing to _____?" he asked slyly.   1 mark

19   "That meal was _____!" exclaimed Mia. "Thank you!"   1 mark

20   _____ to the Met Office, a terrible storm is on its way.   1 mark

    Test Administrator Transcript 4 on page 38

1 "Don't judge me too _____," pleaded the villain. 1 mark

2 Ivan handled the _____ stamp with great care. 1 mark

3 Fiona is attending her first job _____ next week. 1 mark

4 Olivia is one of the most _____ people I know. 1 mark

5 Pizza is Gemma's least _____ food. 1 mark

6 _____ membership at the gym costs £75 a month. 1 mark

7 The minister had an _____ meeting with union leaders. 1 mark

8 When I was younger, I played in a chamber _____. 1 mark

9 Cheryl was in the _____ position of being on holiday. 1 mark

10 Both armies _____ long and hard. 1 mark

11 Look at the time; it is almost a _____ past midnight! 1 mark

12 Vinnie dropped his _____ in his coffee. 1 mark

13 Francesca couldn't believe how _____ Sarah had been. 1 mark

14 We do not particularly like the new school _____. 1 mark

15 Whilst very heavy, _____ is surprisingly soft. 1 mark

16 Lilly got her _____ caught in the door. 1 mark

17 Some locals discovered the tomb entirely by _____. 1 mark

18 "That bag doesn't belong to me; _____ Jane's," said Jo. 1 mark

19 The tourists waved _____ at us as we rode by. 1 mark

20 Professor Xavier's _____ shocked us all. 1 mark

1 Janice is one of our most _____ students.   1 mark

2 _____ all over the world have condemned this move.   1 mark

3 The country's _____ were redrawn after the war.   1 mark

4 The heavy _____ train rumbled down the tracks.   1 mark

5 Several illegal _____ were found in the suspect's home.   1 mark

6 The dark _____ were infested with rats.   1 mark

7 Hal sat on the porch, _____ his guitar.   1 mark

8 As this passport has expired, it is _____.   1 mark

9 Misha swims fifty _____ in the pool every day.   1 mark

10 These notes will provide you with additional _____.   1 mark

11 The Sahara is the largest hot _____ in the world.   1 mark

12 Despite being over ninety, Olga is _____ and hearty.   1 mark

13 A perfectionist will often be _____ with their work.   1 mark

14 I don't like the idea of taking out a bank _____.   1 mark

15 "You have no reason to be _____," Emma assured Liam.   1 mark

16 Adriana uses her local _____ a great deal.   1 mark

17 That theory was _____ by scientists years ago.   1 mark

18 Katie hung a bunch of _____ in the hall.   1 mark

19 Bobby and Nancy are visiting _____ uncle today.   1 mark

20 "Irma's room is an utter pig _____!" exclaimed Neil.   1 mark

Test Administrator Transcript 6 on page 39

1 Regular _____ exercise is part of a healthy lifestyle. | 1 mark

2 The piranha is an _____, carnivorous freshwater fish. | 1 mark

3 Experience has taught Nat to be _____ of large dogs. | 1 mark

4 The sheriff arrested a group of _____ outlaws. | 1 mark

5 The _____ tried, but failed, to fix my desk lamp. | 1 mark

6 Rosa has a dental appointment on the _____. | 1 mark

7 The court ladies dabbed their eyes with their _____. | 1 mark

8 Egyptologists have discovered a pet _____. | 1 mark

9 Mr Mendez is going to stand in our mayoral _____. | 1 mark

10 "Mind your own _____!" shouted Kelly rudely. | 1 mark

11 "It will take a lot of hard work to _____ this," said Pip. | 1 mark

12 Our local _____ centre has a squash court. | 1 mark

13 The _____ is preparing to announce its new policies. | 1 mark

14 A _____-driven limousine drew up outside the gate. | 1 mark

15 I am a great fan of Matisse, _____ his later work. | 1 mark

16 Jack is going to a three-day _____ in Manchester. | 1 mark

17 Feta cheese is a _____ ingredient of Greek salad. | 1 mark

18 The day after _____ is my best friend's birthday. | 1 mark

19 Iris found she had an _____ urge to laugh. | 1 mark

20 Lee is very picky and always finds something to _____. | 1 mark

1   The British Library's _____ of books is immense.   1 mark

2   On _____, Celia spends the weekend in Glasgow.   1 mark

3   Before speaking to the crowd, Omar cleared his _____.   1 mark

4   "That was the _____ peach I've ever had!" declared Kim.   1 mark

5   Our products contain no _____ ingredients.   1 mark

6   We all arrived at the same _____.   1 mark

7   "So, what's on the _____ for supper?" Mark inquired.   1 mark

8   The thick, acrid smoke made it very difficult to _____.   1 mark

9   The concert has been postponed _____.   1 mark

10 My parents never _____ me from asking questions.   1 mark

11 Juan _____ the chance to grab the microphone.   1 mark

12 Strings of _____ lights had been hung on the trees.   1 mark

13 Gina _____ the teacher's question.   1 mark

14 Sean and Quinn have confirmed _____ coming tonight.   1 mark

15 Many people demand _____ replies to their emails.   1 mark

16 The angry _____ shouted at the reckless driver.   1 mark

17 _____, the company no longer offers that service.   1 mark

18 The Santiago family had a _____ time in Hong Kong.   1 mark

19 Evelyn made some chocolate-chip _____ yesterday.   1 mark

20 Petra has an _____ fear of cobwebs.   1 mark

Test Administrator Transcript 8 on page 40

1   Eventually, the criminal's _____ made him confess.   1 mark

2   We _____ many goods from Europe.   1 mark

3   "These accusations are _____!" fumed Mr Brown.   1 mark

4   A _____ is a female sheep.   1 mark

5   People's _____ are a deeply personal matter.   1 mark

6   "You must stir the potion _____," instructed the witch.   1 mark

7   None of Carmen's clothes were on their _____.   1 mark

8   There were at least twenty _____ in Adam's paragraph.   1 mark

9   Make sure you give your article an interesting _____!   1 mark

10   Thick, hot waves of _____ slid down the hill.   1 mark

11   The most _____ thing happened to Emily last week.   1 mark

12   The teacher told the children to sit in a _____.   1 mark

13   The _____ pain in his feet was caused by the cold.   1 mark

14   I need something to _____ to the award ceremony.   1 mark

15   We should all be concerned about levels of _____.   1 mark

16   Wendy's party was a _____; everything went wrong.   1 mark

17   The farmer discovered a Viking _____ buried in his field.   1 mark

18   Khaled always buys his _____ of bread from the bakery.   1 mark

19   Sylvia didn't like any of the film's _____.   1 mark

20   _____ are commonly associated with Christmas.   1 mark

PRACTICE TEST PAPER 10

1 Zelda is making a _____ effort to work harder.   <u>1 mark</u>

2 Everyone fell silent as the _____ entered the Great Hall.   <u>1 mark</u>

3 Dina has promised to give me her _____ for brownies.   <u>1 mark</u>

4 Starlings are known to _____ other kinds of birds.   <u>1 mark</u>

5 Omar hunted _____ for his car keys.   <u>1 mark</u>

6 Tina slung her rucksack over her left _____ and set off.   <u>1 mark</u>

7 We need new _____ for our school's science lab.   <u>1 mark</u>

8 Many cities are now terribly _____.   <u>1 mark</u>

9 Our new TV won't _____ as much space as our old one.   <u>1 mark</u>

10 An _____ amount of money has been spent on this.   <u>1 mark</u>

11 Freya owns at least _____ books about Russia.   <u>1 mark</u>

12 An angry _____ of goblins swarmed over the hill.   <u>1 mark</u>

13 Dr David is a highly respected member of his _____.   <u>1 mark</u>

14 Much to his shame, Tim _____ his cousin's name.   <u>1 mark</u>

15 We would greatly _____ your help in this matter.   <u>1 mark</u>

16 After eating two whole pizzas, Susan felt rather _____.   <u>1 mark</u>

17 Microsoft have released a new operating _____.   <u>1 mark</u>

18 The known facts do not _____ with Bill's statement.   <u>1 mark</u>

19 My grandparents live on a quiet _____ street.   <u>1 mark</u>

20 Many people have become victims of _____ theft.   <u>1 mark</u>

14

1 Unlike Chris, Dennis does not find puppies _____. *1 mark*

2 They stood and stared in awe at the _____ landscape. *1 mark*

3 Draw two circles that _____. *1 mark*

4 Nick has had a nasty _____ for over a month now. *1 mark*

5 The exhibition will end on the _____ of October. *1 mark*

6 "I've no idea _____ I've put my glasses," said Mina. *1 mark*

7 Tracey has finally _____ her fear of water. *1 mark*

8 Ira decided to move to a remote Caribbean _____. *1 mark*

9 The deer was attacked by a pair of _____ wolves. *1 mark*

10 The gentle _____ of jasmine filled the room. *1 mark*

11 Nicola _____ her pride and apologised to Fran. *1 mark*

12 "What will life be like in the 22nd _____?" I wondered. *1 mark*

13 "I have nothing _____ to say," stated the politician. *1 mark*

14 The witch's warning kept _____ in Sir Tristan's mind. *1 mark*

15 None of the Trojans heeded Cassandra's _____. *1 mark*

16 More _____ can be found on our website. *1 mark*

17 The magician made the rabbit _____ into thin air. *1 mark*

18 "There is always room for _____," Mr Singh said. *1 mark*

19 _____ are not nearly as common as they used to be. *1 mark*

20 The generals _____ a plan to ensure their victory. *1 mark*

Test Administrator Transcript 11 on page 42

1 The _____ of church bells sounded across the valley. 1 mark

2 The new president had no _____ for corrupt ministers. 1 mark

3 Pete said that he was _____ to believe Kevin's tale. 1 mark

4 Atoms and molecules are types of _____ particles. 1 mark

5 _____ of any kind should be done away with. 1 mark

6 Mr Sterne challenged Mr Butterworth to a _____. 1 mark

7 During the _____, you may purchase refreshments. 1 mark

8 To betray one's _____ is the height of disloyalty. 1 mark

9 Sunlight can _____ affect a person's mood. 1 mark

10 Care should be taken when operating heavy _____. 1 mark

11 Several _____ had been chained to the iron railings. 1 mark

12 The dead hero's body was placed on a funeral _____. 1 mark

13 Leaves commonly cause _____ to the train service. 1 mark

14 The Three _____ figure prominently in Greek legends. 1 mark

15 I've _____ how much money I owe Marina. 1 mark

16 As the water _____ was old, it had to be replaced. 1 mark

17 The tube was _____ with tired commuters. 1 mark

18 Many people do not like to admit to being _____. 1 mark

19 The king's gold _____ was encrusted with diamonds. 1 mark

20 A _____ wolf is a person who is very independent. 1 mark

Test Administrator Transcript 12 on page 43

1   "That is an _____ idea!" said Ahmed, smiling.   1 mark

2   People are often fooled by get-rich-quick _____.   1 mark

3   Make sure your answer contains only _____ information.   1 mark

4   I've always wanted to visit a Moroccan _____.   1 mark

5   Please leave a message with my _____ if I'm not in.   1 mark

6   Unfortunately, this product is not _____ at this time.   1 mark

7   Several _____ have erupted on islands in the Pacific.   1 mark

8   A prime number is only _____ by itself and 1.   1 mark

9   They had a _____ time at Mr Magnificent's Circus.   1 mark

10   Ashish's stories of his holiday were highly _____.   1 mark

11   Mr Bennett vowed to remain a _____ all his life.   1 mark

12   I need to buy some _____ currency before I travel.   1 mark

13   You must _____ this image in order to use it.   1 mark

14   Try as we might, we could not _____ Lucas to join us.   1 mark

15   A plaque marks the place where the _____ died.   1 mark

16   Bees _____ with each other through dance.   1 mark

17   Do not attempt to open any packages that look _____.   1 mark

18   A slender _____ moon hung in the night sky.   1 mark

19   "Please, don't _____ me when I'm talking," said Julie.   1 mark

20   Two words that _____ are 'blue' and 'true'.   1 mark

1 The film star made a _____ apology to his fans. — *1 mark*

2 Rather _____, I thought Sal would do the right thing. — *1 mark*

3 The contents of this letter are _____. — *1 mark*

4 Just then, a _____ shriek cut through the silent woods. — *1 mark*

5 The candle gradually melted into a _____ lump of wax. — *1 mark*

6 Yonas and I are going to _____ on a science project. — *1 mark*

7 These regulations are not _____ to you. — *1 mark*

8 "This process is _____," warned the scientist. — *1 mark*

9 Today, we learnt about the importance of dental _____. — *1 mark*

10 Daisy does not like her father's _____. — *1 mark*

11 Harry did not have the _____ to argue with Una. — *1 mark*

12 The knight eyed his _____ warily. — *1 mark*

13 The groom adjusted the horse's _____. — *1 mark*

14 Salads can be both tasty and _____. — *1 mark*

15 "I am sure _____ just a rumour," Layla replied. — *1 mark*

16 Jimmy's dog, Cindy, is terribly _____. — *1 mark*

17 _____ she was very tired, Selma stayed up until midnight. — *1 mark*

18 You should always be _____ careful when using knives. — *1 mark*

19 I am helping to paint the _____ for our school play. — *1 mark*

20 The tailor took Lord Randall's _____ for his new suit. — *1 mark*

1   Sophie's testimony was not _____ in court.   <u>1 mark</u>

2   "I've left your laptop in sleep _____," Ross said.   <u>1 mark</u>

3   The town used to be home to three Victorian _____.   <u>1 mark</u>

4   We had our PE lesson in the _____ as it was raining.   <u>1 mark</u>

5   Enormous crystal _____ lit the palace's ballroom.   <u>1 mark</u>

6   I've yet to see the new iPhone _____.   <u>1 mark</u>

7   _____ is a mineral made of silicon and oxygen.   <u>1 mark</u>

8   Eddie stared at the _____; they made no sense at all.   <u>1 mark</u>

9   Uncle Fred enjoys going to historical _____.   <u>1 mark</u>

10   As she never caused any _____, Mel was an ideal tenant.   <u>1 mark</u>

11   King Arthur refused to heed Merlin's wise _____.   <u>1 mark</u>

12   During his speech, Gary made _____ to his boyhood.   <u>1 mark</u>

13   After she was done, Angela put the _____ in the drawer.   <u>1 mark</u>

14   Len's _____ that I come to the party was tiresome.   <u>1 mark</u>

15   This submarine can carry up to 18 _____.   <u>1 mark</u>

16   As the earth becomes warmer, more _____ are likely.   <u>1 mark</u>

17   Al Capone was an _____ Chicago gangster.   <u>1 mark</u>

18   Bernard was both attracted to and _____ by the snake.   <u>1 mark</u>

19   Melissa raised her hand to _____ a taxi.   <u>1 mark</u>

20   The children soon became _____ with their new nanny.   <u>1 mark</u>

1 "At ten pounds, that bag is a _____," Rania noted. 1 mark

2 Police are carrying out a _____ search of the area. 1 mark

3 I can't read Jumana's _____; it's just a scribble! 1 mark

4 The Silk Road is the name of a very old trade _____. 1 mark

5 Please reply at your earliest possible _____. 1 mark

6 Although _____, the child was remarkably wise. 1 mark

7 Dramatic bolts of _____ lit up the overcast sky. 1 mark

8 I always think that _____ look rather sad. 1 mark

9 Khaled has joined the local _____ theatre company. 1 mark

10 Aunt Matilda is kindly _____ to take us to the museum. 1 mark

11 Parents often unknowingly _____ their teenage children. 1 mark

12 Pythagoras believed in the _____ of souls. 1 mark

13 An interesting _____ about Mexico is on tonight. 1 mark

14 Our _____ grows marrows in her garden. 1 mark

15 What is the difference between perfume and _____? 1 mark

16 Sherlock Holmes was _____ to solve the mystery. 1 mark

17 The brontosaurus was a _____ dinosaur. 1 mark

18 Make sure there is a _____ amount of oil in the pan. 1 mark

19 "Put that back on the shelf _____!" thundered Mo. 1 mark

20 The athlete was _____ because he had cheated. 1 mark

Test Administrator Transcript 16 on page 46

1   This plant has many _____ uses.   1 mark

2   My new watch is _____ to heat as well as water.   1 mark

3   The _____ vizier plotted against the Sultan.   1 mark

4   The quality of that plumber's work is _____.   1 mark

5   "What a _____! I'm moving to York too," said Raja.   1 mark

6   The new town hall is being designed by a young _____.   1 mark

7   On a _____ weekday, Tony goes to bed at 10 o'clock.   1 mark

8   The _____ of the Stuart monarchs are very eventful.   1 mark

9   _____ are small, black, dried seedless grapes.   1 mark

10   "Luckily, this is just a _____ wound," said the doctor.   1 mark

11   "That's a _____ nonsensical idea!" spluttered Mira.   1 mark

12   This car is _____ with all the latest gadgets.   1 mark

13   Our weekend plans are _____ on the weather.   1 mark

14   A lady was handing out holiday _____ at the station.   1 mark

15   Lydia was rather _____ that we didn't go with her.   1 mark

16   These Edwardian dolls are highly _____.   1 mark

17   Try to draw a _____ line without a ruler.   1 mark

18   "You, sir, are nothing but a _____," said Lady Arundel.   1 mark

19   I can't _____ of a time without the internet.   1 mark

20   My tests are causing me a great deal of _____.   1 mark

1 After the snow, conditions on the roads were _____. 1 mark

2 "I don't think that's a _____ option," said Frank. 1 mark

3 Anna was shocked to learn she was _____ to a fortune. 1 mark

4 The _____ between the two brothers was striking. 1 mark

5 Dom _____ us that he'd taken care of everything. 1 mark

6 There used to be 20 _____ at our old school. 1 mark

7 The ship sank slowly until it became entirely _____. 1 mark

8 "I've _____ £100 to your account," Helen said. 1 mark

9 _____ SIM phones are useful for regular travellers. 1 mark

10 A _____ is a doctor who has direct contact with patients. 1 mark

11 A member of a powerful crime _____ has been caught. 1 mark

12 An ornate _____ mirror hung over the fireplace. 1 mark

13 The Lincolns have had their fair share of _____. 1 mark

14 _____ is sometimes used as a treatment. 1 mark

15 Does anyone know how many _____ there are? 1 mark

16 As the school bell _____, the students headed inside. 1 mark

17 This _____ can be used to make cookies and pastry. 1 mark

18 The family was fooled by the _____ stranger. 1 mark

19 Blake wants to train to be a _____ when he is older. 1 mark

20 Ro's whispers were so quiet they were almost _____. 1 mark

Test Administrator Transcript 18 on page 47

1   The exhausted _____ fell asleep within minutes.   1 mark

2   The RSPCA works to prevent the _____ of animals.   1 mark

3   They say that _____ is a sign of intelligence.   1 mark

4   The Battle of Trafalgar is a famous British _____ victory.   1 mark

5   I generally find _____ soup quite bland.   1 mark

6   The _____ deadline for all entries is next Thursday.   1 mark

7   The news is _____ depressing.   1 mark

8   Alex has been up all night; he looks a total _____!   1 mark

9   "My _____ is clear," stated Sir Alfred defiantly.   1 mark

10   The judge _____ spoke to the members of the jury.   1 mark

11   As a child, Ian tended to _____ everything.   1 mark

12   The king hosted a _____ in honour of his guests.   1 mark

13   "Which dessert would you _____?" Steve asked.   1 mark

14   On _____, we go to the cinema twice a month.   1 mark

15   The life _____ of a horse is between 25 and 30 years.   1 mark

16   A central lunar eclipse does not _____ very often.   1 mark

17   He's terribly _____: he tells everyone how clever he is.   1 mark

18   Scientists are trying to _____ new types of fuel.   1 mark

19   It is _____ that we resolve this problem now.   1 mark

20   These activists have endured years of _____.   1 mark

Test Administrator Transcript 19 on page 48

1   Vicky _____ agreed to help Ivy prepare her speech.   1 mark

2   Having a pet can be a _____ burden.   1 mark

3   The word _____ originates in the late 19th century.   1 mark

4   The general will _____ his troops shortly.   1 mark

5   Linus wore a _____ helmet to the fancy-dress party!   1 mark

6   Many _____ are in danger of becoming extinct.   1 mark

7   I'm not quite sure what a _____ looks like.   1 mark

8   The diameter of a circle passes through its _____.   1 mark

9   The balloon made its gradual _____ over the hills.   1 mark

10 Can you think of any _____ to mobile phones?   1 mark

11 "We try to make the past _____," said the historian.   1 mark

12 Far from being _____, the referee was clearly biased.   1 mark

13 Getting a university _____ is now very expensive.   1 mark

14 The children were intrigued by the duck-billed _____.   1 mark

15 Heba always has a _____ hanging on her kitchen wall.   1 mark

16 The hero made a _____ of silly mistakes.   1 mark

17 A _____ is a tropical storm in the Northwest Pacific.   1 mark

18 Sadly, many _____ practices still occur all over the world.   1 mark

19 Chizzy is not that _____ when it comes to food.   1 mark

20 The school _____ announced his retirement.   1 mark

Test Administrator Transcript 20 on page 49

1 Rameses II is famous for having numerous _____.   1 mark

2 Although somewhat _____, the jute bag was sturdy.   1 mark

3 The words 'dull' and 'boring' are _____.   1 mark

4 "So, Doctor. What's the _____?" inquired Matt.   1 mark

5 The news that we had the day off school was a _____.   1 mark

6 This wire must be kept _____ at all times.   1 mark

7 We were each given a _____ chocolate after our meal.   1 mark

8 There are glaring _____ in the company's report.   1 mark

9 Every Saturday morning, my granddad _____ the lawn.   1 mark

10 The secret agent was _____ into enemy territory.   1 mark

11 _____ patterns have a distinct appeal.   1 mark

12 "Your grades are _____ low," said the teacher.   1 mark

13 Vince found the _____ quite disgusting.   1 mark

14 The sculptor _____ away at a piece of granite.   1 mark

15 The directions Sheila gave me were terribly _____.   1 mark

16 _____ medicine must be taken by mouth.   1 mark

17 "My _____ is beyond question!" declared the soldier.   1 mark

18 "I'm afraid these files are _____," Irene told Tim.   1 mark

19 I was amazed at how _____ the forest vegetation was.   1 mark

20 Ben lives on the sixteenth _____ of a tower block.   1 mark

1 The _____ elves hid the knight's armour.   1 mark

2 The _____ of the coastline is what gives it its charm.   1 mark

3 Parents may _____ their child if they wish.   1 mark

4 The Smiths are celebrating their wedding _____.   1 mark

5 "That _____ is unique," observed the archaeologist.   1 mark

6 When Sonia walked in, the room became _____ quieter.   1 mark

7 This manuscript is priceless: it is the only one in _____.   1 mark

8 The children were delighted by the _____ of acrobats.   1 mark

9 We _____ apologise for any inconvenience caused.   1 mark

10 Teddy can do some amazing tricks with a _____.   1 mark

11 I hate to say this, but my uncle's cooking is _____.   1 mark

12 If you don't know what a word means, use your _____.   1 mark

13 The new factory will help to ease local _____.   1 mark

14 The _____ Greeks created many wonderful things.   1 mark

15 Siobhan has written the _____ to a poetry anthology.   1 mark

16 We _____ to leave now, or we'll miss our train.   1 mark

17 To serve one's country is a great _____ and honour.   1 mark

18 The writer has denied that his new novel is _____.   1 mark

19 The academic _____ have dismissed this report.   1 mark

20 The millionaire's _____ sailed into the harbour.   1 mark

Test Administrator Transcript 22 on page 50

1   The _____ sat motionless on a large rock.   <u>1 mark</u>

2   Mrs Philips was surprisingly _____ with us.   <u>1 mark</u>

3   "_____ is the best policy," quipped the thief.   <u>1 mark</u>

4   Despite his _____ appearance, the ogre was kindly.   <u>1 mark</u>

5   Jamila runs an _____ shop on the High Road.   <u>1 mark</u>

6   Make sure you put the soap and the food in _____ bags.   <u>1 mark</u>

7   Charlie _____ to Argentina twenty years ago.   <u>1 mark</u>

8   My father finds local _____ politics very frustrating.   <u>1 mark</u>

9   If you bring your receipt with you, we will _____ you.   <u>1 mark</u>

10   Dr Trevor prescribed a course of _____ for Emily.   <u>1 mark</u>

11   The company has been ordered to pay a _____ fine.   <u>1 mark</u>

12   _____, I don't drink coffee after midday.   <u>1 mark</u>

13   Molly was granted an _____ as she'd been ill.   <u>1 mark</u>

14   "What *are* you doing?!" _____ Thomas.   <u>1 mark</u>

15   Catherine refused to _____ to her opponent.   <u>1 mark</u>

16   Owing to his _____, the employee was fired.   <u>1 mark</u>

17   At the heart of this novel lies a terrifying _____.   <u>1 mark</u>

18   Richard paused _____ before answering the question.   <u>1 mark</u>

19   Insomnia can be a _____ of anxiety.   <u>1 mark</u>

20   There are far too many _____ on TV nowadays.   <u>1 mark</u>

PRACTICE TEST PAPER 24

1   A _____ is found at the beginning of a book.   *1 mark*

2   Works by Turner are much _____ after by collectors.   *1 mark*

3   Only some types of _____ can be eaten.   *1 mark*

4   Graham's explanation was nothing short of _____.   *1 mark*

5   The politician apologised for her _____ in judgement.   *1 mark*

6   _____ objects are objects that are not alive, like stones.   *1 mark*

7   "That vase looks very _____ there," observed Lola.   *1 mark*

8   These old photographs are _____.   *1 mark*

9   Over the years, the sea had _____ the cliffs.   *1 mark*

10   Mr Huntley has been a _____ for seven years now.   *1 mark*

11   The Jurassic Period _____ the Cretaceous Period.   *1 mark*

12   Many planets, like Mars, are named after _____ beings.   *1 mark*

13   Wolves are among the most _____ of animals.   *1 mark*

14   This year, our school _____ will be held in Prince's Park.   *1 mark*

15   I don't care if these shoes are _____; they're comfortable!   *1 mark*

16   The base angles of an _____ triangle are equal.   *1 mark*

17   Planting trees encourages natural _____.   *1 mark*

18   The two sisters made a secret _____.   *1 mark*

19   Wilma started laughing _____ and couldn't stop.   *1 mark*

20   Working with _____ is both rewarding and challenging.   *1 mark*

1   "The cast's performance was _____," said the critic.   1 mark

2   The soaring _____ affected us all badly.   1 mark

3   The piazza was monitored by several _____ cameras.   1 mark

4   At Annie's Cafe, we _____ your complete satisfaction!   1 mark

5   The locket contained a _____ portrait.   1 mark

6   "Make the most of this _____," advised Merlin.   1 mark

7   The speed of _____ change nowadays is dizzying.   1 mark

8   Elsa found she'd been given a _____ ten pound note.   1 mark

9   They've cancelled all the flights for no _____ reason.   1 mark

10   We believe that a shift in public opinion is _____.   1 mark

11   Elizabeth II is now Britain's longest-ruling _____.   1 mark

12   These _____ are home to several vintage airplanes.   1 mark

13   The ice has made many country roads _____.   1 mark

14   I can't stand promotional emails; they're a real _____.   1 mark

15   The army has declared _____ law after days of unrest.   1 mark

16   An unmarked _____ pulled up outside the bank.   1 mark

17   We stayed in a luxurious _____ in a hotel in Venice.   1 mark

18   The workers are suing the management for _____.   1 mark

19   The _____ surrounding this film is growing.   1 mark

20   At school today, we learnt about _____.   1 mark

Test Administrator Transcript 25 on page 52

1 The nation is _____ the loss of their beloved leader. 1 mark

2 Having a pet is a good way to teach a child about _____. 1 mark

3 This film requires considerable _____ of disbelief. 1 mark

4 "Help me," the wounded soldier said _____. 1 mark

5 The situation should be _____ in light of these changes. 1 mark

6 Reena has started learning to play the _____. 1 mark

7 _____ bicycles are easy to store. 1 mark

8 "I think Tom's stories are wholly _____," said Fiona. 1 mark

9 These riots have created _____ in the capital city. 1 mark

10 Olive Avenue runs _____ to Anson Road. 1 mark

11 Carol usually gives the _____ of being content. 1 mark

12 Our aunt has made a _____ amount of food for us. 1 mark

13 Dan is being _____ by requests to change his mind. 1 mark

14 The defiant town was _____ by the invading army. 1 mark

15 I was bitten by _____ when I went to Italy last summer. 1 mark

16 The generous donor wishes to remain _____. 1 mark

17 "Such insolence is not to be _____!" snapped the duke. 1 mark

18 An area of high _____ is moving towards the UK. 1 mark

19 The young _____ amused herself by making up songs. 1 mark

20 _____ reports say the president is about to resign. 1 mark

1 Farida's aunt is an _____ physicist. 1 mark

2 _____ typically causes a lot of coughing. 1 mark

3 Feeling _____, Betty disobeyed her parents. 1 mark

4 Natasha _____ to the temptation of a piece of cake. 1 mark

5 The _____ of Winchester is attending the event. 1 mark

6 Kit has been a member of our hockey _____ since 2004. 1 mark

7 Hussein waved his hand _____ at my objections. 1 mark

8 There was, Idris pointed out _____, another solution. 1 mark

9 The police are building a _____ profile of the criminal. 1 mark

10 The team showed their true _____ during the last match. 1 mark

11 The arch was adorned with _____ carved figures. 1 mark

12 The goblins made every effort to _____ the king's plans. 1 mark

13 Dr Jekyll spent long days and nights in his _____. 1 mark

14 "Such action would be _____," Ameena warned. 1 mark

15 "What are _____ used for?" asked Niall. 1 mark

16 Angie has _____ against poverty for many years. 1 mark

17 Taylor threw down his tennis _____ in a fit of anger. 1 mark

18 Learning he had lied to her, Juan's mother was _____. 1 mark

19 Serena felt _____ after a relaxing weekend. 1 mark

20 Linda's _____ in Japanese is truly remarkable. 1 mark

1 The word _____ means the human mind, soul, or spirit. 1 mark

2 Millie groaned as she saw the length of the _____. 1 mark

3 The librarian trawled through the _____ to find the letter. 1 mark

4 I've started drinking _____ tea. 1 mark

5 The knight began to _____ the blunt blade of his dagger. 1 mark

6 Sayida has won this year's creative writing _____. 1 mark

7 Raja bought his _____ a goldfish for her birthday. 1 mark

8 Computers can have a _____ impact on children's learning. 1 mark

9 After all the hype, the film itself was an _____. 1 mark

10 Kitty _____ some sweets from the corner shop. 1 mark

11 Higher interest rates can be a _____ to recovery. 1 mark

12 These pears make a nice _____ to blue cheese. 1 mark

13 _____ is an important, if difficult, aspect of poetry. 1 mark

14 "These are recent _____," observed the anthropologist. 1 mark

15 The effects of global warming could be _____. 1 mark

16 "I cannot stress the _____ of this enough," Lewis said. 1 mark

17 "What is lost is found," said the soothsayer _____. 1 mark

18 People's _____ will vary according to their dialect. 1 mark

19 The _____ of knowledge is becoming increasingly digital. 1 mark

20 _____ artistic differences often cause bands to break up. 1 mark

Test Administrator Transcript 28 on page 54

1   Some protesters have been making _____ remarks.   <u>1 mark</u>

2   Is the date of this document _____ from its contents?   <u>1 mark</u>

3   The products were recalled as they had been _____.   <u>1 mark</u>

4   No one can stand Carl; he's so _____!   <u>1 mark</u>

5   The visitors were enchanted by the _____ French village.   <u>1 mark</u>

6   The _____ light bulb flickered as it came on.   <u>1 mark</u>

7   _____ Sam Riley is hoping for a promotion.   <u>1 mark</u>

8   Some animals have a complex social _____.   <u>1 mark</u>

9   The word _____ means following a logical order.   <u>1 mark</u>

10   The opposition claimed the election was _____.   <u>1 mark</u>

11   Our football club was _____ at the end of last season.   <u>1 mark</u>

12   "Okay," Kyle said _____ to his sister. "You're right."   <u>1 mark</u>

13   "This is a very _____ way of doing things," said Fred.   <u>1 mark</u>

14   "My hair looks _____!" complained Elizabeth.   <u>1 mark</u>

15   On Tuesday, Ralph is going to see his _____.   <u>1 mark</u>

16   "Mrs Bentu is extremely _____," noted Viv.   <u>1 mark</u>

17   Arwa pulled the _____ over her head and went to sleep.   <u>1 mark</u>

18   The kind-hearted prince gave _____ to the poor.   <u>1 mark</u>

19   Scotland recently held an independence _____.   <u>1 mark</u>

20   The Ice Queen's beauty had a distinctly _____ quality.   <u>1 mark</u>

PRACTICE TEST PAPER 30

1 Most atomic _____ consist of neutrons and protons.   1 mark

2 The illness left him with an unhealthy, _____ complexion.   1 mark

3 If something is _____, it is related to the sense of hearing.   1 mark

4 It would be _____ of me to say I regret it; I don't.   1 mark

5 Some people's _____ to the flu is higher than others.   1 mark

6 Despite her _____ appetite, Pamela is very skinny.   1 mark

7 People aged under 30 are _____ for this offer.   1 mark

8 We were all taken aback by Shady's _____.   1 mark

9 Ghosts that are noisy are called _____.   1 mark

10 Lucy _____ the wet towel out in the sink.   1 mark

11 Otto works as a _____ at an investment company.   1 mark

12 The MP's speech was dismissed as empty _____.   1 mark

13 The sum of two _____ angles is 90 degrees.   1 mark

14 Pierre shivered at the demon's fierce, _____ stare.   1 mark

15 "Oooh! You scared me!" _____ Miranda.   1 mark

16 Who was the _____ of last year's Man Booker Prize?   1 mark

17 Lady Earlham gasped at her daughter's _____.   1 mark

18 The search for _____ lifeforms goes on.   1 mark

19 It would be _____ of us not to visit our friends.   1 mark

20 _____ are heavy, broad knives.   1 mark

Test Administrator Transcript 30 on page 56

ADMINISTERING & MARKING THE SPELLING TESTS

ADMINISTERING THE SPELLING TESTS

- The **Spelling Tests** in this book **need to be read out loud** to the student from **the transcripts** provided in the following pages.

- Each spelling test should take around 15 minutes, but can take longer if need be.

- Before administering each spelling test, read out the following instructions:

  * *Listen carefully to these instructions.*
  * *There are 20 sentences in your test paper. Each sentence has a word missing from it.*
  * *I will first read the missing word on its own. Then, I will read the whole sentence with the missing word in it. Finally, I will read the missing word again on its own.*
  * *I will do this each time for each sentence.*
  * *Listen carefully to the missing word and write it in the space provided in your test paper.*
  * *Make sure you spell the word correctly.*

- Answer any questions the student may have before proceeding with the test.

- In the Transcripts, there are entries such as the one below:

  *Spelling 1: The word is **delighted**.*
  *Sam was **delighted** with his present.*
  *The word is **delighted**.*

- These should be read out to the student in the following manner:

  * *Read out loud: "Spelling number 1."*
  * *Read out loud: "The word is delighted."*
  * *Read out loud: "Sam was delighted with his present."*
  * *Read out loud: "The word is delighted."*

- Leave a gap of at least 12 seconds between each spelling.
- At the end, read all 20 sentences out again in order from the beginning.
- Give the student time to change any of their answers if they wish.
- When the test is over, say "This is the end of the test."

MARKING THE SPELLING TESTS

- Each **correctly spelt word** is worth **1 mark**.
- Half marks **are not to be awarded**.
- If a word requires a **capital letter, an apostrophe,** or **a hyphen**, these punctuation marks **must be used correctly** by the student **for the mark to be awarded**.
- Spellings that have been written as **two distinct** or **incorrectly hyphenated** words **cannot be accepted**.

TEST ADMINISTRATOR TRANSCRIPT 1

Spelling 1: The word is **category**.
This book falls into the **category** of historical fiction.
The word is **category**.

Spelling 2: The word is **recognised**.
We all **recognised** the seriousness of the situation.
The word is **recognised**.

Spelling 3: The word is **individual**.
The man who lives upstairs is an odd **individual**.
The word is **individual**.

Spelling 4: The word is **micro-organisms**.
Micro-organisms are found in almost all natural habitats.
The word is **micro-organisms**.

Spelling 5: The word is **environment**.
Recycling is clearly good for the **environment**.
The word is **environment**.

Spelling 6: The word is **alter**.
The wealthy merchant was forced to **alter** his will.
The word is **alter**.

Spelling 7: The word is **bruise**.
"I've got a massive **bruise** on my arm," whined Ian.
The word is **bruise**.

Spelling 8: The word is **illogical**.
"That is utterly **illogical**!" scoffed Ravi.
The word is **illogical**.

Spelling 9: The word is **language**.
Being able to speak a second **language** can be very useful.
The word is **language**.

Spelling 10: The word is **engineer**.
Nadine's father is a famous civil **engineer**.
The word is **engineer**.

Spelling 11: The word is **suggest**.
"Might I **suggest** the onion soup, sir?" said the waiter.
The word is **suggest**.

Spelling 12: The word is **definite**.
There is a **definite** change in Polly's attitude.
The word is **definite**.

Spelling 13: The word is **babysitter**.
"I'm too old for a **babysitter**!" complained Jan.
The word is **babysitter**.

Spelling 14: The word is **injustice**.
Vera cried at the **injustice** of being wrongly blamed.
The word is **injustice**.

Spelling 15: The word is **familiar**.
"That lady looks **familiar**," mused Kate.
The word is **familiar**.

Spelling 16: The word is **repetitious**.
The twins' story was terrible as it was so **repetitious**.
The word is **repetitious**.

Spelling 17: The word is **deceived**.
The crooked lawyer **deceived** many of his clients.
The word is **deceived**.

Spelling 18: The word is **accommodate**.
The hotel is happy to **accommodate** guests with pets.
The word is **accommodate**.

Spelling 19: The word is **democratically**.
That government wasn't **democratically** elected.
The word is **democratically**.

Spelling 20: The word is **muscle**.
The most hard-working **muscle** is the heart.
The word is **muscle**.

TEST ADMINISTRATOR TRANSCRIPT 2

Spelling 1: The word is **treasure**.
The pirates hid their stolen **treasure** in a Cornish cave.
The word is **treasure**.

Spelling 2: The word is **who's**.
"**Who's** responsible for this mess?" demanded the cook.
The word is **who's**.

Spelling 3: The word is **critic**.
That **critic** never gives new writers good reviews.
The word is **critic**.

Spelling 4: The word is **lamb**.
Tina loved her grandmother's **lamb** stew.
The word is **lamb**.

Spelling 5: The word is **magically**.
The fairy made the knight's knapsack **magically** vanish.
The word is **magically**.

Spelling 6: The word is **special**.
You need a **special** screwdriver for that.
The word is **special**.

Spelling 7: The word is **doubt**.
I have no **doubt** that our team will win their match.
The word is **doubt**.

Spelling 8: The word is **Wednesday**.
Last **Wednesday**, Jeff didn't go to work because he was ill.
The word is **Wednesday**.

Spelling 9: The word is **profit**.
Our local community will **profit** from these changes.
The word is **profit**.

Spelling 10: The word is **allowed**.
Parking is not **allowed** in this area.
The word is **allowed**.

Spelling 11: The word is **misbehaved**.
Will is being punished because he **misbehaved** at school.
The word is **misbehaved**.

Spelling 12: The word is **except**.
Except for Helena, we all went on the class trip.
The word is **except**.

Spelling 13: The word is **cautious**.
Margaret is a very **cautious** driver.
The word is **cautious**.

Spelling 14: The word is **cereal**.
Many people have a bowl of **cereal** for breakfast.
The word is **cereal**.

Spelling 15: The word is **charity**.
Lulu works for a **charity** shop in Devon.
The word is **charity**.

Spelling 16: The word is **tough**.
The customer complained that her steak was too **tough**.
The word is **tough**.

Spelling 17: The word is **height**.
The teacher lined the students up in order of **height**.
The word is **height**.

Spelling 18: The word is **disgrace**.
"Your fingernails are a **disgrace**," grumbled Tom's mother.
The word is **disgrace**.

Spelling 19: The word is **preventable**.
Tragically, this disaster was **preventable**.
The word is **preventable**.

Spelling 20: The word is **incorrect**.
The assumption that Shakespeare wrote this is **incorrect**.
The word is **incorrect**.

TEST ADMINISTRATOR TRANSCRIPT 3

Spelling 1: The word is **council**.
The **council** has promised to look into this matter.
The word is **council**.

Spelling 2: The word is **story**.
The children found the **story** a bit dull.

The word is **story**.

Spelling 3: The word is **waltz**.
The **waltz** used to be a very popular dance.
The word is **waltz**.

Spelling 4: The word is **delightful**.
"A cup of hot cocoa sounds positively **delightful**!" said Val.
The word is **delightful**.

Spelling 5: The word is **grammar**.
I find Latin **grammar** rather confusing.
The word is **grammar**.

Spelling 6: The word is **mishandled**.
Alan feels that Josh **mishandled** the situation.
The word is **mishandled**.

Spelling 7: The word is **gnome**.
Rita has bought a new **gnome** for her garden.
The word is **gnome**.

Spelling 8: The word is **literally**.
The word **literally** is misused all the time.
The word is **literally**.

Spelling 9: The word is **international**.
Some people think London needs a new **international** airport.
The word is **international**.

Spelling 10: The word is **lessen**.
"Drink this; it will help **lessen** the pain," said the nurse.
The word is **lessen**.

Spelling 11: The word is **invisible**.
Lemon juice can be used as a kind of **invisible** ink.
The word is **invisible**.

Spelling 12: The word is **bizarre**.
The **bizarre** events that followed stunned everyone.
The word is **bizarre**.

Spelling 13: The word is **chorus**.
My favourite part of that song is the **chorus**.
The word is **chorus**.

Spelling 14: The word is **deselect**.
Deselect option 2 if you do not wish us to email you.
The word is **deselect**.

Spelling 15: The word is **peel**.
Could you **peel** these oranges, please?
The word is **peel**.

Spelling 16: The word is **impossibly**.
Clara's new kitten is **impossibly** cute.
The word is **impossibly**.

Spelling 17: The word is **anchovies**.

I dislike **anchovies**, but I love sardines.
The word is **anchovies**.

Spelling 18: The word is **glamorous**.
My aunt was very **glamorous** when she was in her twenties.
The word is **glamorous**.

Spelling 19: The word is **course**.
Molly is taking a Spanish **course**.
The word is **course**.

Spelling 20: The word is **beige**.
"I think you'd look nice in that **beige** jacket," said Jim.
The word is **beige**.

TEST ADMINISTRATOR TRANSCRIPT 4

Spelling 1: The word is **parliament**.
A group of owls is called a **parliament** of owls.
The word is **parliament**.

Spelling 2: The word is **disapproval**.
The headmaster shook his head slowly in **disapproval**.
The word is **disapproval**.

Spelling 3: The word is **acknowledge**.
Please **acknowledge** your receipt of this email.
The word is **acknowledge**.

Spelling 4: The word is **awkward**.
An **awkward** silence settled over the audience.
The word is **awkward**.

Spelling 5: The word is **impatient**.
Hugo gets very **impatient** when he is hungry.
The word is **impatient**.

Spelling 6: The word is **stomach**.
I can't **stomach** apple juice; it makes me feel sick.
The word is **stomach**.

Spelling 7: The word is **restaurant**.
La Traviata is the most expensive **restaurant** in Milan.
The word is **restaurant**.

Spelling 8: The word is **bough**.
A magpie landed on the uppermost **bough** of the tree.
The word is **bough**.

Spelling 9: The word is **committee**.
Next Monday, the **committee** will meet to discuss this.
The word is **committee**.

Spelling 10: The word is **decision**.
"I've made my **decision**," declared Rufus stubbornly.
The word is **decision**.

Spelling 11: The word is **variety**.
A wide **variety** of fresh fruit was on sale in the canteen.
The word is **variety**.

Spelling 12: The word is **quarts**.
You will need two **quarts** of milk to make the sauce.
The word is **quarts**.

Spelling 13: The word is **explanation**.
Disa gave no **explanation** for her week-long absence.
The word is **explanation**.

Spelling 14: The word is **attached**.
Ted **attached** a recent photograph to the form.
The word is **attached**.

Spelling 15: The word is **flimsy**.
Even though these sandals look **flimsy**, they aren't.
The word is **flimsy**.

Spelling 16: The word is **interfere**.
"Don't **interfere**," snapped Jorge. "I know what to do."
The word is **interfere**.

Spelling 17: The word is **heroine**.
I found the **heroine** in that book rather irritating.
The word is **heroine**.

Spelling 18: The word is **sacrifice**.
"What would you be willing to **sacrifice**?" he asked slyly.
The word is **sacrifice**.

Spelling 19: The word is **delicious**.
"That meal was **delicious**!" exclaimed Mia. "Thank you!"
The word is **delicious**.

Spelling 20: The word is **according**.
According to the Met Office, a terrible storm is on its way.
The word is **according**.

TEST ADMINISTRATOR TRANSCRIPT 5

Spelling 1: The word is **harshly**.
"Don't judge me too **harshly**," pleaded the villain.
The word is **harshly**.

Spelling 2: The word is **precious**.
Ivan handled the **precious** stamp with great care.
The word is **precious**.

Spelling 3: The word is **interview**.
Fiona is attending her first job **interview** next week.
The word is **interview**.

Spelling 4: The word is **reliable**.
Olivia is one of the most **reliable** people I know.
The word is **reliable**.

Spelling 5: The word is **favourite**.
Pizza is Gemma's least **favourite** food.
The word is **favourite**.

Spelling 6: The word is **temporary**.
Temporary membership at the gym costs £75 a month.

The word is **temporary**.

Spelling 7: The word is **informal**.
The minister had an **informal** meeting with union leaders.
The word is **informal**.

Spelling 8: The word is **orchestra**.
When I was younger, I played in a chamber **orchestra**.
The word is **orchestra**.

Spelling 9: The word is **enviable**.
Cheryl was in the **enviable** position of being on holiday.
The word is **enviable**.

Spelling 10: The word is **fought**.
Both armies **fought** long and hard.
The word is **fought**.

Spelling 11: The word is **quarter**.
Look at the time; it is almost a **quarter** past midnight!
The word is **quarter**.

Spelling 12: The word is **biscuit**.
Vinnie dropped his **biscuit** in his coffee.
The word is **biscuit**.

Spelling 13: The word is **impolite**.
Francesca couldn't believe how **impolite** Sarah had been.
The word is **impolite**.

Spelling 14: The word is **chef**.
We do not particularly like the new school **chef**.
The word is **chef**.

Spelling 15: The word is **lead**.
Whilst very heavy, **lead** is surprisingly soft.
The word is **lead**.

Spelling 16: The word is **thumb**.
Lilly got her **thumb** caught in the door.
The word is **thumb**.

Spelling 17: The word is **accident**.
Some locals discovered the tomb entirely by **accident**.
The word is **accident**.

Spelling 18: The word is **it's**.
"That bag doesn't belong to me; **it's** Jane's," said Jo.
The word is **it's**.

Spelling 19: The word is **cheerily**.
The tourists waved **cheerily** at us as we rode by.
The word is **cheerily**.

Spelling 20: The word is **reaction**.
Professor Xavier's **reaction** shocked us all.
The word is **reaction**.

Spelling 1: The word is **diligent**.
Janice is one of our most **diligent** students.
The word is **diligent**.

Spelling 2: The word is **scholars**.
Scholars all over the world have condemned this move.
The word is **scholars**.

Spelling 3: The word is **borders**.
The country's **borders** were redrawn after the war.
The word is **borders**.

Spelling 4: The word is **freight**.
The heavy **freight** train rumbled down the tracks.
The word is **freight**.

Spelling 5: The word is **substances**.
Several illegal **substances** were found in the suspect's home.
The word is **substances**.

Spelling 6: The word is **alleys**.
The dark **alleys** were infested with rats.
The word is **alleys**.

Spelling 7: The word is **strumming**.
Hal sat on the porch, **strumming** his guitar.
The word is **strumming**.

Spelling 8: The word is **invalid**.
As this passport has expired, it is **invalid**.
The word is **invalid**.

Spelling 9: The word is **laps**.
Misha swims fifty **laps** in the pool every day.
The word is **laps**.

Spelling 10: The word is **guidance**.
These notes will provide you with additional **guidance**.
The word is **guidance**.

Spelling 11: The word is **desert**.
The Sahara is the largest hot **desert** in the world.
The word is **desert**.

Spelling 12: The word is **hale**.
Despite being over ninety, Olga is **hale** and hearty.
The word is **hale**.

Spelling 13: The word is **unsatisfied**.
A perfectionist will often be **unsatisfied** with their work.
The word is **unsatisfied**.

Spelling 14: The word is **loan**.
I don't like the idea of taking out a bank **loan**.
The word is **loan**.

Spelling 15: The word is **jealous**.
"You have no reason to be **jealous**," Emma assured Liam.
The word is **jealous**.

Spelling 16: The word is **library**.
Adriana uses her local **library** a great deal.
The word is **library**.

Spelling 17: The word is **discarded**.
That theory was **discarded** by scientists years ago.
The word is **discarded**.

Spelling 18: The word is **mistletoe**.
Katie hung a bunch of **mistletoe** in the hall.
The word is **mistletoe**.

Spelling 19: The word is **their**.
Bobby and Nancy are visiting **their** uncle today.
The word is **their**.

Spelling 20: The word is **sty**.
"Irma's room is an utter pig **sty**!" exclaimed Neil.
The word is **sty**.

TEST ADMINISTRATOR TRANSCRIPT 7

Spelling 1: The word is **physical**.
Regular **physical** exercise is part of a healthy lifestyle.
The word is **physical**.

Spelling 2: The word is **aggressive**.
The piranha is an **aggressive**, carnivorous freshwater fish.
The word is **aggressive**.

Spelling 3: The word is **wary**.
Experience has taught Nat to be **wary** of large dogs.
The word is **wary**.

Spelling 4: The word is **desperate**.
The sheriff arrested a group of **desperate** outlaws.
The word is **desperate**.

Spelling 5: The word is **electrician**.
The **electrician** tried, but failed, to fix my desk lamp.
The word is **electrician**.

Spelling 6: The word is **twelfth**.
Rosa has a dental appointment on the **twelfth**.
The word is **twelfth**.

Spelling 7: The word is **handkerchiefs**.
The court ladies dabbed their eyes with their **handkerchiefs**.
The word is **handkerchiefs**.

Spelling 8: The word is **cemetery**.
Egyptologists have discovered a pet **cemetery**.
The word is **cemetery**.

Spelling 9: The word is **election**.
Mr Mendez is going to stand in our mayoral **election**.

The word is **election**.

Spelling 10: The word is **business**.
"Mind your own **business**!" shouted Kelly rudely.
The word is **business**.

Spelling 11: The word is **achieve**.
"It will take a lot of hard work to **achieve** this," said Pip.
The word is **achieve**.

Spelling 12: The word is **leisure**.
Our local **leisure** centre has a squash court.
The word is **leisure**.

Spelling 13: The word is **government**.
The **government** is preparing to announce its new policies.
The word is **government**.

Spelling 14: The word is **chauffeur**.
A **chauffeur**-driven limousine drew up outside the gate.
The word is **chauffeur**.

Spelling 15: The word is **especially**.
I am a great fan of Matisse, **especially** his later work.
The word is **especially**.

Spelling 16: The word is **conference**.
Jack is going to a three-day **conference** in Manchester.
The word is **conference**.

Spelling 17: The word is **necessary**.
Feta cheese is a **necessary** ingredient of Greek salad.
The word is **necessary**.

Spelling 18: The word is **tomorrow**.
The day after **tomorrow** is my best friend's birthday.
The word is **tomorrow**.

Spelling 19: The word is **irresistible**.
Iris found she had an **irresistible** urge to laugh.
The word is **irresistible**.

Spelling 20: The word is **criticise**.
Lee is very picky and always finds something to **criticise**.
The word is **criticise**.

TEST ADMINISTRATOR TRANSCRIPT 8

Spelling 1: The word is **catalogue**.
The British Library's **catalogue** of books is immense.
The word is **catalogue**.

Spelling 2: The word is **occasion**.
On **occasion**, Celia spends the weekend in Glasgow.
The word is **occasion**.

Spelling 3: The word is **throat**.
Before speaking to the crowd, Omar cleared his **throat**.
The word is **throat**.

Spelling 4: The word is **juiciest**.
"That was the **juiciest** peach I've ever had!" declared Kim.
The word is **juiciest**.

Spelling 5: The word is **artificial**.
Our products contain no **artificial** ingredients.
The word is **artificial**.

Spelling 6: The word is **conclusion**.
We all arrived at the same **conclusion**.
The word is **conclusion**.

Spelling 7: The word is **menu**.
"So, what's on the **menu** for supper?" Mark inquired.
The word is **menu**.

Spelling 8: The word is **breathe**.
The thick, acrid smoke made it very difficult to **breathe**.
The word is **breathe**.

Spelling 9: The word is **indefinitely**.
The concert has been postponed **indefinitely**.
The word is **indefinitely**.

Spelling 10: The word is **discouraged**.
My parents never **discouraged** me from asking questions.
The word is **discouraged**.

Spelling 11: The word is **seized**.
Juan **seized** the chance to grab the microphone.
The word is **seized**.

Spelling 12: The word is **coloured**.
Strings of **coloured** lights had been hung on the trees.
The word is **coloured**.

Spelling 13: The word is **misheard**.
Gina **misheard** the teacher's question.
The word is **misheard**.

Spelling 14: The word is **they're**.
Sean and Quinn have confirmed **they're** coming tonight.
The word is **they're**.

Spelling 15: The word is **immediate**.
Many people demand **immediate** replies to their emails.
The word is **immediate**.

Spelling 16: The word is **cyclist**.
The angry **cyclist** shouted at the reckless driver.
The word is **cyclist**.

Spelling 17: The word is **regrettably**.
Regrettably, the company no longer offers that service.
The word is **regrettably**.

Spelling 18: The word is **fabulous**.
The Santiago family had a **fabulous** time in Hong Kong.
The word is **fabulous**.

Spelling 19: The word is **cookies**.
Evelyn made some chocolate-chip **cookies** yesterday.
The word is **cookies**.

Spelling 20: The word is **irrational**.
Petra has an **irrational** fear of cobwebs.
The word is **irrational**.

TEST ADMINISTRATOR TRANSCRIPT 9

Spelling 1: The word is **guilt**.
Eventually, the criminal's **guilt** made him confess.
The word is **guilt**.

Spelling 2: The word is **import**.
We **import** many goods from Europe.
The word is **import**.

Spelling 3: The word is **outrageous**.
"These accusations are **outrageous**!" fumed Mr Brown.
The word is **outrageous**.

Spelling 4: The word is **ewe**.
A **ewe** is a female sheep.
The word is **ewe**.

Spelling 5: The word is **beliefs**.
People's **beliefs** are a deeply personal matter.
The word is **beliefs**.

Spelling 6: The word is **clockwise**.
"You must stir the potion **clockwise**," instructed the witch.
The word is **clockwise**.

Spelling 7: The word is **hangers**.
None of Carmen's clothes were on their **hangers**.
The word is **hangers**.

Spelling 8: The word is **misspellings**.
There were at least twenty **misspellings** in Adam's paragraph.
The word is **misspellings**.

Spelling 9: The word is **subheading**.
Make sure you give your article an interesting **subheading**!
The word is **subheading**.

Spelling 10: The word is **lava**.
Thick, hot waves of **lava** slid down the hill.
The word is **lava**.

Spelling 11: The word is **extraordinary**.
The most **extraordinary** thing happened to Emily last week.
The word is **extraordinary**.

Spelling 12: The word is **semicircle**.
The teacher told the children to sit in a **semicircle**.
The word is **semicircle**.

Spelling 13: The word is **unbearable**.

The **unbearable** pain in his feet was caused by the cold.
The word is **unbearable**.

Spelling 14: The word is **wear**.
I need something to **wear** to the award ceremony.
The word is **wear**.

Spelling 15: The word is **pollution**.
We should all be concerned about levels of **pollution**.
The word is **pollution**.

Spelling 16: The word is **fiasco**.
Wendy's party was a **fiasco**; everything went wrong.
The word is **fiasco**.

Spelling 17: The word is **hoard**.
The farmer discovered a Viking **hoard** buried in his field.
The word is **hoard**.

Spelling 18: The word is **loaves**.
Khaled always buys his **loaves** of bread from the bakery.
The word is **loaves**.

Spelling 19: The word is **characters**.
Sylvia didn't like any of the film's **characters**.
The word is **characters**.

Spelling 20: The word is **reindeer**.
Reindeer are commonly associated with Christmas.
The word is **reindeer**.

TEST ADMINISTRATOR TRANSCRIPT 10

Spelling 1: The word is **conscious**.
Zelda is making a **conscious** effort to work harder.
The word is **conscious**.

Spelling 2: The word is **empress**.
Everyone fell silent as the **empress** entered the Great Hall.
The word is **empress**.

Spelling 3: The word is **recipe**.
Dina has promised to give me her **recipe** for brownies.
The word is **recipe**.

Spelling 4: The word is **harass**.
Starlings are known to **harass** other kinds of birds.
The word is **harass**.

Spelling 5: The word is **frantically**.
Omar hunted **frantically** for his car keys.
The word is **frantically**.

Spelling 6: The word is **shoulder**.
Tina slung her rucksack over her left **shoulder** and set off.
The word is **shoulder**.

Spelling 7: The word is **equipment**.
We need new **equipment** for our school's science lab.
The word is **equipment**.

Spelling 8: The word is **overpopulated**.
Many cities are now terribly **overpopulated**.
The word is **overpopulated**.

Spelling 9: The word is **occupy**.
Our new TV won't **occupy** as much space as our old one.
The word is **occupy**.

Spelling 10: The word is **unimaginable**.
An **unimaginable** amount of money has been spent on this.
The word is **unimaginable**.

Spelling 11: The word is **forty**.
Freya owns at least **forty** books about Russia.
The word is **forty**.

Spelling 12: The word is **horde**.
An angry **horde** of goblins swarmed over the hill.
The word is **horde**.

Spelling 13: The word is **profession**.
Dr David is a highly respected member of his **profession**.
The word is **profession**.

Spelling 14: The word is **misremembered**.
Much to his shame, Tim **misremembered** his cousin's name.
The word is **misremembered**.

Spelling 15: The word is **appreciate**.
We would greatly **appreciate** your help in this matter.
The word is **appreciate**.

Spelling 16: The word is **queasy**.
After eating two whole pizzas, Susan felt rather **queasy**.
The word is **queasy**.

Spelling 17: The word is **system**.
Microsoft have released a new operating **system**.
The word is **system**.

Spelling 18: The word is **correspond**.
The known facts do not **correspond** with Bill's statement.
The word is **correspond**.

Spelling 19: The word is **residential**.
My grandparents live on a quiet **residential** street.
The word is **residential**.

Spelling 20: The word is **identity**.
Many people have become victims of **identity** theft.
The word is **identity**.

TEST ADMINISTRATOR TRANSCRIPT 11

Spelling 1: The word is **adorable**.
Unlike Chris, Dennis does not find puppies **adorable**.
The word is **adorable**.

Spelling 2: The word is **mountainous**.
They stood and stared in awe at the **mountainous** landscape.
The word is **mountainous**.

Spelling 3: The word is **intersect**.
Draw two circles that **intersect**.
The word is **intersect**.

Spelling 4: The word is **cough**.
Nick has had a nasty **cough** for over a month now.
The word is **cough**.

Spelling 5: The word is **eighth**.
The exhibition will end on the **eighth** of October.
The word is **eighth**.

Spelling 6: The word is **where**.
"I've no idea **where** I've put my glasses," said Mina.
The word is **where**.

Spelling 7: The word is **conquered**.
Tracey has finally **conquered** her fear of water.
The word is **conquered**.

Spelling 8: The word is **isle**.
Ira decided to move to a remote Caribbean **isle**.
The word is **isle**.

Spelling 9: The word is **vicious**.
The deer was attacked by a pair of **vicious** wolves.
The word is **vicious**.

Spelling 10: The word is **fragrance**.
The gentle **fragrance** of jasmine filled the room.
The word is **fragrance**.

Spelling 11: The word is **swallowed**.
Nicola **swallowed** her pride and apologised to Fran.
The word is **swallowed**.

Spelling 12: The word is **century**.
"What will life be like in the 22nd **century**?" I wondered.
The word is **century**.

Spelling 13: The word is **further**.
"I have nothing **further** to say," stated the politician.
The word is **further**.

Spelling 14: The word is **echoing**.
The witch's warning kept **echoing** in Sir Tristan's mind.
The word is **echoing**.

Spelling 15: The word is **prophecy**.
None of the Trojans heeded Cassandra's **prophecy**.
The word is **prophecy**.

Spelling 16: The word is **information**.
More **information** can be found on our website.
The word is **information**.

Spelling 17: The word is **disappear**.
The magician made the rabbit **disappear** into thin air.
The word is **disappear**.

Spelling 18: The word is **improvement**.
"There is always room for **improvement**," Mr Singh said.
The word is **improvement**.

Spelling 19: The word is **cheques**.
Cheques are not nearly as common as they used to be.
The word is **cheques**.

Spelling 20: The word is **devised**.
The generals **devised** a plan to ensure their victory.
The word is **devised**.

TEST ADMINISTRATOR TRANSCRIPT 12

Spelling 1: The word is **peal**.
The **peal** of church bells sounded across the valley.
The word is **peal**.

Spelling 2: The word is **tolerance**.
The new president had no **tolerance** for corrupt ministers.
The word is **tolerance**.

Spelling 3: The word is **inclined**.
Pete said that he was **inclined** to believe Kevin's tale.
The word is **inclined**.

Spelling 4: The word is **microscopic**.
Atoms and molecules are types of **microscopic** particles.
The word is **microscopic**.

Spelling 5: The word is **inequality**.
Inequality of any kind should be done away with.
The word is **inequality**.

Spelling 6: The word is **duel**.
Mr Sterne challenged Mr Butterworth to a **duel**.
The word is **duel**.

Spelling 7: The word is **intermission**.
During the **intermission**, you may purchase refreshments.
The word is **intermission**.

Spelling 8: The word is **allies**.
To betray one's **allies** is the height of disloyalty.
The word is **allies**.

Spelling 9: The word is **tangibly**.
Sunlight can **tangibly** affect a person's mood.
The word is **tangibly**.

Spelling 10: The word is **machinery**.
Care should be taken when operating heavy **machinery**.
The word is **machinery**.

Spelling 11: The word is **bicycles**.
Several **bicycles** had been chained to the iron railings.

The word is **bicycles**.

Spelling 12: The word is **pyre**.
The dead hero's body was placed on a funeral **pyre**.
The word is **pyre**.

Spelling 13: The word is **disruptions**.
Leaves commonly cause **disruptions** to the train service.
The word is **disruptions**.

Spelling 14: The word is **Fates**.
The Three **Fates** figure prominently in Greek legends.
The word is **Fates**.

Spelling 15: The word is **miscalculated**.
I've **miscalculated** how much money I owe Marina.
The word is **miscalculated**.

Spelling 16: The word is **trough**.
As the water **trough** was old, it had to be replaced.
The word is **trough**.

Spelling 17: The word is **packed**.
The tube was **packed** with tired commuters.
The word is **packed**.

Spelling 18: The word is **superstitious**.
Many people do not like to admit to being **superstitious**.
The word is **superstitious**.

Spelling 19: The word is **sceptre**.
The king's gold **sceptre** was encrusted with diamonds.
The word is **sceptre**.

Spelling 20: The word is **lone**.
A **lone** wolf is a person who is very independent.
The word is **lone**.

TEST ADMINISTRATOR TRANSCRIPT 13

Spelling 1: The word is **excellent**.
"That is an **excellent** idea!" said Ahmed, smiling.
The word is **excellent**.

Spelling 2: The word is **schemes**.
People are often fooled by get-rich-quick **schemes**.
The word is **schemes**.

Spelling 3: The word is **relevant**.
Make sure your answer contains only **relevant** information.
The word is **relevant**.

Spelling 4: The word is **bazaar**.
I've always wanted to visit a Moroccan **bazaar**.
The word is **bazaar**.

Spelling 5: The word is **secretary**.
Please leave a message with my **secretary** if I'm not in.
The word is **secretary**.

Spelling 6: The word is **available**.
Unfortunately, this product is not **available** at this time.
The word is **available**.

Spelling 7: The word is **volcanoes**.
Several **volcanoes** have erupted on islands in the Pacific.
The word is **volcanoes**.

Spelling 8: The word is **divisible**.
A prime number is only **divisible** by itself and 1.
The word is **divisible**.

Spelling 9: The word is **marvellous**.
They had a **marvellous** time at Mr Magnificent's Circus.
The word is **marvellous**.

Spelling 10: The word is **improbable**.
Ashish's stories of his holiday were highly **improbable**.
The word is **improbable**.

Spelling 11: The word is **bachelor**.
Mr Bennett vowed to remain a **bachelor** all his life.
The word is **bachelor**.

Spelling 12: The word is **foreign**.
I need to buy some **foreign** currency before I travel.
The word is **foreign**.

Spelling 13: The word is **license**.
You must **license** this image in order to use it.
The word is **license**.

Spelling 14: The word is **persuade**.
Try as we might, we could not **persuade** Lucas to join us.
The word is **persuade**.

Spelling 15: The word is **martyr**.
A plaque marks the place where the **martyr** died.
The word is **martyr**.

Spelling 16: The word is **communicate**.
Bees **communicate** with each other through dance.
The word is **communicate**.

Spelling 17: The word is **suspicious**.
Do not attempt to open any packages that look **suspicious**.
The word is **suspicious**.

Spelling 18: The word is **crescent**.
A slender **crescent** moon hung in the night sky.
The word is **crescent**.

Spelling 19: The word is **interrupt**.
"Please, don't **interrupt** me when I'm talking," said Julie.
The word is **interrupt**.

Spelling 20: The word is **rhyme**.
Two words that **rhyme** are 'blue' and 'true'.
The word is **rhyme**.

TEST ADMINISTRATOR TRANSCRIPT 14

Spelling 1: The word is **sincere**.
The film star made a **sincere** apology to his fans.
The word is **sincere**.

Spelling 2: The word is **naively**.
Rather **naively**, I thought Sal would do the right thing.
The word is **naively**.

Spelling 3: The word is **confidential**.
The contents of this letter are **confidential**.
The word is **confidential**.

Spelling 4: The word is **piercing**.
Just then, a **piercing** shriek cut through the silent woods.
The word is **piercing**.

Spelling 5: The word is **misshapen**.
The candle gradually melted into a **misshapen** lump of wax.
The word is **misshapen**.

Spelling 6: The word is **collaborate**.
Yonas and I are going to **collaborate** on a science project.
The word is **collaborate**.

Spelling 7: The word is **applicable**.
These regulations are not **applicable** to you.
The word is **applicable**.

Spelling 8: The word is **irreversible**.
"This process is **irreversible**," warned the scientist.
The word is **irreversible**.

Spelling 9: The word is **hygiene**.
Today, we learnt about the importance of dental **hygiene**.
The word is **hygiene**.

Spelling 10: The word is **moustache**.
Daisy does not like her father's **moustache**.
The word is **moustache**.

Spelling 11: The word is **strength**.
Harry did not have the **strength** to argue with Una.
The word is **strength**.

Spelling 12: The word is **foe**.
The knight eyed his **foe** warily.
The word is **foe**.

Spelling 13: The word is **bridle**.
The groom adjusted the horse's **bridle**.
The word is **bridle**.

Spelling 14: The word is **nutritious**.
Salads can be both tasty and **nutritious**.
The word is **nutritious**.

Spelling 15: The word is **that's**.
"I am sure **that's** just a rumour," Layla replied.
The word is **that's**.

Spelling 16: The word is **disobedient**.
Jimmy's dog, Cindy, is terribly **disobedient**.
The word is **disobedient**.

Spelling 17: The word is **although**.
Although she was very tired, Selma stayed up until midnight.
The word is **although**.

Spelling 18: The word is **extremely**.
You should always be **extremely** careful when using knives.
The word is **extremely**.

Spelling 19: The word is **scenery**.
I am helping to paint the **scenery** for our school play.
The word is **scenery**.

Spelling 20: The word is **measurements**.
The tailor took Lord Randall's **measurements** for his new suit.
The word is **measurements**.

TEST ADMINISTRATOR TRANSCRIPT 15

Spelling 1: The word is **admissible**.
Sophie's testimony was not **admissible** in court.
The word is **admissible**.

Spelling 2: The word is **mode**.
"I've left your laptop in sleep **mode**," Ross said.
The word is **mode**.

Spelling 3: The word is **distilleries**.
The town used to be home to three Victorian **distilleries**.
The word is **distilleries**.

Spelling 4: The word is **gymnasium**.
We had our PE lesson in the **gymnasium** as it was raining.
The word is **gymnasium**.

Spelling 5: The word is **chandeliers**.
Enormous crystal **chandeliers** lit the palace's ballroom.
The word is **chandeliers**.

Spelling 6: The word is **advertisement**.
I've yet to see the new iPhone **advertisement**.
The word is **advertisement**.

Spelling 7: The word is **quartz**.
Quartz is a mineral made of silicon and oxygen.
The word is **quartz**.

Spelling 8: The word is **diagrams**.
Eddie stared at the **diagrams**; they made no sense at all.
The word is **diagrams**.

Spelling 9: The word is **re-enactments**.
Uncle Fred enjoys going to historical **re-enactments**.
The word is **re-enactments**.

Spelling 10: The word is **disturbance**.
As she never caused any **disturbance**, Mel was an ideal tenant.
The word is **disturbance**.

Spelling 11: The word is **counsel**.
King Arthur refused to heed Merlin's wise **counsel**.
The word is **counsel**.

Spelling 12: The word is **reference**.
During his speech, Gary made **reference** to his boyhood.
The word is **reference**.

Spelling 13: The word is **scissors**.
After she was done, Angela put the **scissors** in the drawer.
The word is **scissors**.

Spelling 14: The word is **insistence**.
Len's **insistence** that I come to the party was tiresome.
The word is **insistence**.

Spelling 15: The word is **torpedoes**.
This submarine can carry up to 18 **torpedoes**.
The word is **torpedoes**.

Spelling 16: The word is **droughts**.
As the earth becomes warmer, more **droughts** are likely.
The word is **droughts**.

Spelling 17: The word is **infamous**.
Al Capone was an **infamous** Chicago gangster.
The word is **infamous**.

Spelling 18: The word is **repelled**.
Bernard was both attracted to and **repelled** by the snake.
The word is **repelled**.

Spelling 19: The word is **hail**.
Melissa raised her hand to **hail** a taxi.
The word is **hail**.

Spelling 20: The word is **disenchanted**.
The children soon became **disenchanted** with their new nanny.
The word is **disenchanted**.

TEST ADMINISTRATOR TRANSCRIPT 16

Spelling 1: The word is **bargain**.
"At ten pounds, that bag is a **bargain**," Rania noted.
The word is **bargain**.

Spelling 2: The word is **thorough**.
Police are carrying out a **thorough** search of the area.
The word is **thorough**.

Spelling 3: The word is **signature**.
I can't read Jumana's **signature**; it's just a scribble!
The word is **signature**.

Spelling 4: The word is **route**.
The Silk Road is the name of a very old trade **route**.
The word is **route**.

Spelling 5: The word is **convenience**.
Please reply at your earliest possible **convenience**.
The word is **convenience**.

Spelling 6: The word is **illiterate**.
Although **illiterate**, the child was remarkably wise.
The word is **illiterate**.

Spelling 7: The word is **lightning**.
Dramatic bolts of **lightning** lit up the overcast sky.
The word is **lightning**.

Spelling 8: The word is **rhinoceroses**.
I always think that **rhinoceroses** look rather sad.
The word is **rhinoceroses**.

Spelling 9: The word is **amateur**.
Khaled has joined the local **amateur** theatre company.
The word is **amateur**.

Spelling 10: The word is **offering**.
Aunt Matilda is kindly **offering** to take us to the museum.
The word is **offering**.

Spelling 11: The word is **embarrass**.
Parents often unknowingly **embarrass** their teenage children.
The word is **embarrass**.

Spelling 12: The word is **reincarnation**.
Pythagoras believed in the **reincarnation** of souls.
The word is **reincarnation**.

Spelling 13: The word is **programme**.
An interesting **programme** about Mexico is on tonight.
The word is **programme**.

Spelling 14: The word is **neighbour**.
Our **neighbour** grows marrows in her garden.
The word is **neighbour**.

Spelling 15: The word is **cologne**.
What is the difference between perfume and **cologne**?
The word is **cologne**.

Spelling 16: The word is **determined**.
Sherlock Holmes was **determined** to solve the mystery.
The word is **determined**.

Spelling 17: The word is **herbivorous**.
The brontosaurus was a **herbivorous** dinosaur.
The word is **herbivorous**.

Spelling 18: The word is **sufficient**.
Make sure there is a **sufficient** amount of oil in the pan.
The word is **sufficient**.

Spelling 19: The word is **immediately**.
"Put that back on the shelf **immediately**!" thundered Mo.
The word is **immediately**.

Spelling 20: The word is **disqualified**.
The athlete was **disqualified** because he had cheated.
The word is **disqualified**.

TEST ADMINISTRATOR TRANSCRIPT 17

Spelling 1: The word is **medicinal**.
This plant has many **medicinal** uses.
The word is **medicinal**.

Spelling 2: The word is **resistant**.
My new watch is **resistant** to heat as well as water.
The word is **resistant**.

Spelling 3: The word is **ambitious**.
The **ambitious** vizier plotted against the Sultan.
The word is **ambitious**.

Spelling 4: The word is **substandard**.
The quality of that plumber's work is **substandard**.
The word is **substandard**.

Spelling 5: The word is **coincidence**.
"What a **coincidence**! I'm moving to York too," said Raja.
The word is **coincidence**.

Spelling 6: The word is **architect**.
The new town hall is being designed by a young **architect**.
The word is **architect**.

Spelling 7: The word is **typical**.
On a **typical** weekday, Tony goes to bed at 10 o'clock.
The word is **typical**.

Spelling 8: The word is **reigns**.
The **reigns** of the Stuart monarchs are very eventful.
The word is **reigns**.

Spelling 9: The word is **currants**.
Currants are small, black, dried seedless grapes.
The word is **currants**.

Spelling 10: The word is **superficial**.
"Luckily, this is just a **superficial** wound," said the doctor.
The word is **superficial**.

Spelling 11: The word is **completely**.
"That's a **completely** nonsensical idea!" spluttered Mira.
The word is **completely**.

Spelling 12: The word is **equipped**.
This car is **equipped** with all the latest gadgets.
The word is **equipped**.

Spelling 13: The word is **dependent**.
Our weekend plans are **dependent** on the weather.
The word is **dependent**.

Spelling 14: The word is **brochures**.
A lady was handing out holiday **brochures** at the station.
The word is **brochures**.

Spelling 15: The word is **disappointed**.
Lydia was rather **disappointed** that we didn't go with her.
The word is **disappointed**.

Spelling 16: The word is **collectible**.
These Edwardian dolls are highly **collectible**.
The word is **collectible**.

Spelling 17: The word is **straight**.
Try to draw a **straight** line without a ruler.
The word is **straight**.

Spelling 18: The word is **rogue**.
"You, sir, are nothing but a **rogue**," said Lady Arundel.
The word is **rogue**.

Spelling 19: The word is **conceive**.
I can't **conceive** of a time without the internet.
The word is **conceive**.

Spelling 20: The word is **anxiety**.
My tests are causing me a great deal of **anxiety**.
The word is **anxiety**.

TEST ADMINISTRATOR TRANSCRIPT 18

Spelling 1: The word is **hazardous**.
After the snow, conditions on the roads were **hazardous**.
The word is **hazardous**.

Spelling 2: The word is **viable**.
"I don't think that's a **viable** option," said Frank.
The word is **viable**.

Spelling 3: The word is **heiress**.
Anna was shocked to learn she was **heiress** to a fortune.
The word is **heiress**.

Spelling 4: The word is **dissimilarity**.
The **dissimilarity** between the two brothers was striking.
The word is **dissimilarity**.

Spelling 5: The word is **reassured**.
Dom **reassured** us that he'd taken care of everything.
The word is **reassured**.

Spelling 6: The word is **boarders**.
There used to be 20 **boarders** at our old school.
The word is **boarders**.

Spelling 7: The word is **submerged**.
The ship sank slowly until it became entirely **submerged**.
The word is **submerged**.

Spelling 8: The word is **transferred**.
"I've **transferred** £100 to your account," Helen said.
The word is **transferred**.

Spelling 9: The word is **dual**.
Dual SIM phones are useful for regular travellers.
The word is **dual**.

Spelling 10: The word is **clinician**.
A **clinician** is a doctor who has direct contact with patients.
The word is **clinician**.

Spelling 11: The word is **syndicate**.
A member of a powerful crime **syndicate** has been caught.
The word is **syndicate**.

Spelling 12: The word is **gilt**.
An ornate **gilt** mirror hung over the fireplace.
The word is **gilt**.

Spelling 13: The word is **crises**.
The Lincolns have had their fair share of **crises**.
The word is **crises**.

Spelling 14: The word is **hypnosis**.
Hypnosis is sometimes used as a treatment.
The word is **hypnosis**.

Spelling 15: The word is **galaxies**.
Does anyone know how many **galaxies** there are?
The word is **galaxies**.

Spelling 16: The word is **tolled**.
As the school bell **tolled**, the students headed inside.
The word is **tolled**.

Spelling 17: The word is **dough**.
This **dough** can be used to make cookies and pastry.
The word is **dough**.

Spelling 18: The word is **charismatic**.
The family was fooled by the **charismatic** stranger.
The word is **charismatic**.

Spelling 19: The word is **commando**.
Blake wants to train to be a **commando** when he is older.
The word is **commando**.

Spelling 20: The word is **inaudible**.
Ro's whispers were so quiet they were almost **inaudible**.
The word is **inaudible**.

TEST ADMINISTRATOR TRANSCRIPT 19

Spelling 1: The word is **soldier**.
The exhausted **soldier** fell asleep within minutes.

The word is **soldier**.

Spelling 2: The word is **mistreatment**.
The RSPCA works to prevent the **mistreatment** of animals.
The word is **mistreatment**.

Spelling 3: The word is **curiosity**.
They say that **curiosity** is a sign of intelligence.
The word is **curiosity**.

Spelling 4: The word is **naval**.
The Battle of Trafalgar is a famous British **naval** victory.
The word is **naval**.

Spelling 5: The word is **vegetable**.
I generally find **vegetable** soup quite bland.
The word is **vegetable**.

Spelling 6: The word is **submission**.
The **submission** deadline for all entries is next Thursday.
The word is **submission**.

Spelling 7: The word is **frequently**.
The news is **frequently** depressing.
The word is **frequently**.

Spelling 8: The word is **wreck**.
Alex has been up all night; he looks a total **wreck**!
The word is **wreck**.

Spelling 9: The word is **conscience**.
"My **conscience** is clear," stated Sir Alfred defiantly.
The word is **conscience**.

Spelling 10: The word is **solemnly**.
The judge **solemnly** spoke to the members of the jury.
The word is **solemnly**.

Spelling 11: The word is **exaggerate**.
As a child, Ian tended to **exaggerate** everything.
The word is **exaggerate**.

Spelling 12: The word is **banquet**.
The king hosted a **banquet** in honour of his guests.
The word is **banquet**.

Spelling 13: The word is **recommend**.
"Which dessert would you **recommend**?" Steve asked.
The word is **recommend**.

Spelling 14: The word is **average**.
On **average**, we go to the cinema twice a month.
The word is **average**.

Spelling 15: The word is **expectancy**.
The life **expectancy** of a horse is between 25 and 30 years.
The word is **expectancy**.

Spelling 16: The word is **occur**.
A central lunar eclipse does not **occur** very often.

The word is **occur**.

Spelling 17: The word is **conceited**.
He's terribly **conceited**: he tells everyone how clever he is.
The word is **conceited**.

Spelling 18: The word is **develop**.
Scientists are trying to **develop** new types of fuel.
The word is **develop**.

Spelling 19: The word is **crucial**.
It is **crucial** that we resolve this problem now.
The word is **crucial**.

Spelling 20: The word is **prejudice**.
These activists have endured years of **prejudice**.
The word is **prejudice**.

TEST ADMINISTRATOR TRANSCRIPT 20

Spelling 1: The word is **readily**.
Vicky **readily** agreed to help Ivy prepare her speech.
The word is **readily**.

Spelling 2: The word is **financial**.
Having a pet can be a **financial** burden.
The word is **financial**.

Spelling 3: The word is **automobile**.
The word **automobile** originates in the late 19th century.
The word is **automobile**.

Spelling 4: The word is **address**.
The general will **address** his troops shortly.
The word is **address**.

Spelling 5: The word is **fireman's**.
Linus wore a **fireman's** helmet to the fancy-dress party!
The word is **fireman's**.

Spelling 6: The word is **species**.
Many **species** are in danger of becoming extinct.
The word is **species**.

Spelling 7: The word is **thistle**.
I'm not quite sure what a **thistle** looks like.
The word is **thistle**.

Spelling 8: The word is **centre**.
The diameter of a circle passes through its **centre**.
The word is **centre**.

Spelling 9: The word is **ascent**.
The balloon made its gradual **ascent** over the hills.
The word is **ascent**.

Spelling 10: The word is **disadvantages**.
Can you think of any **disadvantages** to mobile phones?
The word is **disadvantages**.

Spelling 11: The word is **accessible**.
"We try to make the past **accessible**," said the historian.
The word is **accessible**.

Spelling 12: The word is **impartial**.
Far from being **impartial**, the referee was clearly biased.
The word is **impartial**.

Spelling 13: The word is **education**.
Getting a university **education** is now very expensive.
The word is **education**.

Spelling 14: The word is **platypus**.
The children were intrigued by the duck-billed **platypus**.
The word is **platypus**.

Spelling 15: The word is **calendar**.
Heba always has a **calendar** hanging on her kitchen wall.
The word is **calendar**.

Spelling 16: The word is **series**.
The hero made a **series** of silly mistakes.
The word is **series**.

Spelling 17: The word is **typhoon**.
A **typhoon** is a tropical storm in the Northwest Pacific.
The word is **typhoon**.

Spelling 18: The word is **inhumane**.
Sadly, many **inhumane** practices still occur all over the world.
The word is **inhumane**.

Spelling 19: The word is **adventurous**.
Chizzy is not that **adventurous** when it comes to food.
The word is **adventurous**.

Spelling 20: The word is **principal**.
The school **principal** announced his retirement.
The word is **principal**.

TEST ADMINISTRATOR TRANSCRIPT 21

Spelling 1: The word is **offspring**.
Rameses II is famous for having numerous **offspring**.
The word is **offspring**.

Spelling 2: The word is **coarse**.
Although somewhat **coarse**, the jute bag was sturdy.
The word is **coarse**.

Spelling 3: The word is **synonymous**.
The words 'dull' and 'boring' are **synonymous**.
The word is **synonymous**.

Spelling 4: The word is **diagnosis**.
"So, Doctor. What's the **diagnosis**?" inquired Matt.
The word is **diagnosis**.

Spelling 5: The word is **hoax**.

The news that we had the day off school was a **hoax**.
The word is **hoax**.

Spelling 6: The word is **taut**.
This wire must be kept **taut** at all times.
The word is **taut**.

Spelling 7: The word is **complimentary**.
We were each given a **complimentary** chocolate after our meal.
The word is **complimentary**.

Spelling 8: The word is **omissions**.
There are glaring **omissions** in the company's report.
The word is **omissions**.

Spelling 9: The word is **mowed**.
Every Saturday morning, my granddad **mowed** the lawn.
The word is **mowed**.

Spelling 10: The word is **parachuted**.
The secret agent was **parachuted** into enemy territory.
The word is **parachuted**.

Spelling 11: The word is **asymmetrical**.
Asymmetrical patterns have a distinct appeal.
The word is **asymmetrical**.

Spelling 12: The word is **woefully**.
"Your grades are **woefully** low," said the teacher.
The word is **woefully**.

Spelling 13: The word is **larva**.
Vince found the **larva** quite disgusting.
The word is **larva**.

Spelling 14: The word is **chiselled**.
The sculptor **chiselled** away at a piece of granite.
The word is **chiselled**.

Spelling 15: The word is **imprecise**.
The directions Sheila gave me were terribly **imprecise**.
The word is **imprecise**.

Spelling 16: The word is **oral**.
Oral medicine must be taken by mouth.
The word is **oral**.

Spelling 17: The word is **patriotism**.
"My **patriotism** is beyond question!" declared the soldier.
The word is **patriotism**.

Spelling 18: The word is **irretrievable**.
"I'm afraid these files are **irretrievable**," Irene told Tim.
The word is **irretrievable**.

Spelling 19: The word is **luscious**.
I was amazed at how **luscious** the forest vegetation was.
The word is **luscious**.

Spelling 20: The word is **storey**.
Ben lives on the sixteenth **storey** of a tower block.
The word is **storey**.

TEST ADMINISTRATOR TRANSCRIPT 22

Spelling 1: The word is **mischievous**.
The **mischievous** elves hid the knight's armour.
The word is **mischievous**.

Spelling 2: The word is **irregularity**.
The **irregularity** of the coastline is what gives it its charm.
The word is **irregularity**.

Spelling 3: The word is **accompany**.
Parents may **accompany** their child if they wish.
The word is **accompany**.

Spelling 4: The word is **anniversary**.
The Smiths are celebrating their wedding **anniversary**.
The word is **anniversary**.

Spelling 5: The word is **symbol**.
"That **symbol** is unique," observed the archaeologist.
The word is **symbol**.

Spelling 6: The word is **noticeably**.
When Sonia walked in, the room became **noticeably** quieter.
The word is **noticeably**.

Spelling 7: The word is **existence**.
This manuscript is priceless: it is the only one in **existence**.
The word is **existence**.

Spelling 8: The word is **troupe**.
The children were delighted by the **troupe** of acrobats.
The word is **troupe**.

Spelling 9: The word is **sincerely**.
We **sincerely** apologise for any inconvenience caused.
The word is **sincerely**.

Spelling 10: The word is **gyroscope**.
Teddy can do some amazing tricks with a **gyroscope**.
The word is **gyroscope**.

Spelling 11: The word is **inedible**.
I hate to say this, but my uncle's cooking is **inedible**.
The word is **inedible**.

Spelling 12: The word is **dictionary**.
If you don't know what a word means, use your **dictionary**.
The word is **dictionary**.

Spelling 13: The word is **unemployment**.
The new factory will help to ease local **unemployment**.
The word is **unemployment**.

Spelling 14: The word is **ancient**.

The **ancient** Greeks created many wonderful things.
The word is **ancient**.

Spelling 15: The word is **foreword**.
Siobhan has written the **foreword** to a poetry anthology.
The word is **foreword**.

Spelling 16: The word is **ought**.
We **ought** to leave now, or we'll miss our train.
The word is **ought**.

Spelling 17: The word is **privilege**.
To serve one's country is a great **privilege** and honour.
The word is **privilege**.

Spelling 18: The word is **autobiographical**.
The writer has denied that his new novel is **autobiographical**.
The word is **autobiographical**.

Spelling 19: The word is **community**.
The academic **community** have dismissed this report.
The word is **community**.

Spelling 20: The word is **yacht**.
The millionaire's **yacht** sailed into the harbour.
The word is **yacht**.

TEST ADMINISTRATOR TRANSCRIPT 23

Spelling 1: The word is **chameleon**.
The **chameleon** sat motionless on a large rock.
The word is **chameleon**.

Spelling 2: The word is **lenient**.
Mrs Phillips was surprisingly **lenient** with us.
The word is **lenient**.

Spelling 3: The word is **dishonesty**.
"**Dishonesty** is the best policy," quipped the thief.
The word is **dishonesty**.

Spelling 4: The word is **hideous**.
Despite his **hideous** appearance, the ogre was kindly.
The word is **hideous**.

Spelling 5: The word is **antiques**.
Jamila runs an **antiques** shop on the High Road.
The word is **antiques**.

Spelling 6: The word is **separate**.
Make sure you put the soap and the food in **separate** bags.
The word is **separate**.

Spelling 7: The word is **immigrated**.
Charlie **immigrated** to Argentina twenty years ago.
The word is **immigrated**.

Spelling 8: The word is **borough**.
My father finds local **borough** politics very frustrating.
The word is **borough**.

Spelling 9: The word is **reimburse**.
If you bring your receipt with you, we will **reimburse** you.
The word is **reimburse**.

Spelling 10: The word is **antibiotics**.
Dr Trevor prescribed a course of **antibiotics** for Emily.
The word is **antibiotics**.

Spelling 11: The word is **substantial**.
The company has been ordered to pay a **substantial** fine.
The word is **substantial**.

Spelling 12: The word is **ordinarily**.
Ordinarily, I don't drink coffee after midday.
The word is **ordinarily**.

Spelling 13: The word is **extension**.
Molly was granted an **extension** as she'd been ill.
The word is **extension**.

Spelling 14: The word is **bellowed**.
"What *are* you doing?!" **bellowed** Thomas.
The word is **bellowed**.

Spelling 15: The word is **yield**.
Catherine refused to **yield** to her opponent.
The word is **yield**.

Spelling 16: The word is **misconduct**.
Owing to his **misconduct**, the employee was fired.
The word is **misconduct**.

Spelling 17: The word is **allegory**.
At the heart of this novel lies a terrifying **allegory**.
The word is **allegory**.

Spelling 18: The word is **momentarily**.
Richard paused **momentarily** before answering the question.
The word is **momentarily**.

Spelling 19: The word is **symptom**.
Insomnia can be a **symptom** of anxiety.
The word is **symptom**.

Spelling 20: The word is **commercials**.
There are far too many **commercials** on TV nowadays.
The word is **commercials**.

TEST ADMINISTRATOR TRANSCRIPT 24

Spelling 1: The word is **prologue**.
A **prologue** is found at the beginning of a book.
The word is **prologue**.

Spelling 2: The word is **sought**.
Works by Turner are much **sought** after by collectors.
The word is **sought**.

Spelling 3: The word is **fungi**.
Only some types of **fungi** can be eaten.
The word is **fungi**.

Spelling 4: The word is **implausible**.
Graham's explanation was nothing short of **implausible**.
The word is **implausible**.

Spelling 5: The word is **lapse**.
The politician apologised for her **lapse** in judgement.
The word is **lapse**.

Spelling 6: The word is **inanimate**.
Inanimate objects are objects that are not alive, like stones.
The word is **inanimate**.

Spelling 7: The word is **precarious**.
"That vase looks very **precarious** there," observed Lola.
The word is **precarious**.

Spelling 8: The word is **irreplaceable**.
These old photographs are **irreplaceable**.
The word is **irreplaceable**.

Spelling 9: The word is **eroded**.
Over the years, the sea had **eroded** the cliffs.
The word is **eroded**.

Spelling 10: The word is **widower**.
Mr Huntley has been a **widower** for seven years now.
The word is **widower**.

Spelling 11: The word is **preceded**.
The Jurassic Period **preceded** the Cretaceous Period.
The word is **preceded**.

Spelling 12: The word is **mythological**.
Many planets, like Mars, are named after **mythological** beings.
The word is **mythological**.

Spelling 13: The word is **autonomous**.
Wolves are among the most **autonomous** of animals.
The word is **autonomous**.

Spelling 14: The word is **fete**.*
This year, our school **fete** will be held in Prince's Park.
The word is **fete**.

Spelling 15: The word is **unfashionable**.
I don't care if these shoes are **unfashionable**; they're comfortable!
The word is **unfashionable**.

Spelling 16: The word is **isosceles**.
The base angles of an **isosceles** triangle are equal.
The word is **isosceles**.

Spelling 17: The word is **regeneration**.
Planting trees encourages natural **regeneration**.
The word is **regeneration**.

Spelling 18: The word is **pact**.
The two sisters made a secret **pact**.
The word is **pact**.

Spelling 19: The word is **hysterically**.
Wilma started laughing **hysterically** and couldn't stop.
The word is **hysterically**.

Spelling 20: The word is **colleagues**.
Working with **colleagues** is both rewarding and challenging.
The word is **colleagues**.

TEST ADMINISTRATOR TRANSCRIPT 25

Spelling 1: The word is **inadequate**.
"The cast's performance was **inadequate**," said the critic.
The word is **inadequate**.

Spelling 2: The word is **temperature**.
The soaring **temperature** affected us all badly.
The word is **temperature**.

Spelling 3: The word is **surveillance**.
The piazza was monitored by several **surveillance** cameras.
The word is **surveillance**.

Spelling 4: The word is **guarantee**.
At Annie's Cafe, we **guarantee** your complete satisfaction!
The word is **guarantee**.

Spelling 5: The word is **miniature**.
The locket contained a **miniature** portrait.
The word is **miniature**.

Spelling 6: The word is **opportunity**.
"Make the most of this **opportunity**," advised Merlin.
The word is **opportunity**.

Spelling 7: The word is **technological**.
The speed of **technological** change nowadays is dizzying.
The word is **technological**.

Spelling 8: The word is **counterfeit**.
Elsa found she'd been given a **counterfeit** ten pound note.
The word is **counterfeit**.

Spelling 9: The word is **apparent**.
They've cancelled all the flights for no **apparent** reason.
The word is **apparent**.

Spelling 10: The word is **imminent**.
We believe that a shift in public opinion is **imminent**.
The word is **imminent**.

Spelling 11: The word is **sovereign**.
Elizabeth II is now Britain's longest-ruling **sovereign**.
The word is **sovereign**.

*The word fete may also be correctly spelt fête.

Spelling 12: The word is **hangars**.
These **hangars** are home to several vintage airplanes.
The word is **hangars**.

Spelling 13: The word is **treacherous**.
The ice has made many country roads **treacherous**.
The word is **treacherous**.

Spelling 14: The word is **nuisance**.
I can't stand promotional emails; they're a real **nuisance**.
The word is **nuisance**.

Spelling 15: The word is **martial**.
The army has declared **martial** law after days of unrest.
The word is **martial**.

Spelling 16: The word is **vehicle**.
An unmarked **vehicle** pulled up outside the bank.
The word is **vehicle**.

Spelling 17: The word is **suite**.
We stayed in a luxurious **suite** in a hotel in Venice.
The word is **suite**.

Spelling 18: The word is **negligence**.
The workers are suing the management for **negligence**.
The word is **negligence**.

Spelling 19: The word is **controversy**.
The **controversy** surrounding this film is growing.
The word is **controversy**.

Spelling 20: The word is **photosynthesis**.
At school today, we learnt about **photosynthesis**.
The word is **photosynthesis**.

TEST ADMINISTRATOR TRANSCRIPT 26

Spelling 1: The word is **mourning**.
The nation is **mourning** the loss of their beloved leader.
The word is **mourning**.

Spelling 2: The word is **responsibility**.
Having a pet is a good way to teach a child about **responsibility**.
The word is **responsibility**.

Spelling 3: The word is **suspension**.
This film requires considerable **suspension** of disbelief.
The word is **suspension**.

Spelling 4: The word is **hoarsely**.
"Help me," the wounded soldier said **hoarsely**.
The word is **hoarsely**.

Spelling 5: The word is **re-evaluated**.
The situation should be **re-evaluated** in light of these changes.
The word is **re-evaluated**.

Spelling 6: The word is **tympani**.

Reena has started learning to play the **tympani**.
The word is **tympani**.

Spelling 7: The word is **collapsible**.
Collapsible bicycles are easy to store.
The word is **collapsible**.

Spelling 8: The word is **fictitious**.
"I think Tom's stories are wholly **fictitious**," said Fiona.
The word is **fictitious**.

Spelling 9: The word is **anarchy**.
These riots have created **anarchy** in the capital city.
The word is **anarchy**.

Spelling 10: The word is **parallel**.
Olive Avenue runs **parallel** to Anson Road.
The word is **parallel**.

Spelling 11: The word is **impression**.
Carol usually gives the **impression** of being content.
The word is **impression**.

Spelling 12: The word is **humongous**.
Our aunt has made a **humongous** amount of food for us.
The word is **humongous**.

Spelling 13: The word is **plagued**.
Dan is being **plagued** by requests to change his mind.
The word is **plagued**.

Spelling 14: The word is **besieged**.
The defiant town was **besieged** by the invading army.
The word is **besieged**.

Spelling 15: The word is **mosquitoes**.
I was bitten by **mosquitoes** when I went to Italy last summer.
The word is **mosquitoes**.

Spelling 16: The word is **anonymous**.
The generous donor wishes to remain **anonymous**.
The word is **anonymous**.

Spelling 17: The word is **borne**.
"Such insolence is not to be **borne**!" snapped the duke.
The word is **borne**.

Spelling 18: The word is **pressure**.
An area of high **pressure** is moving towards the UK.
The word is **pressure**.

Spelling 19: The word is **shepherdess**.
The young **shepherdess** amused herself by making up songs.
The word is **shepherdess**.

Spelling 20: The word is **unofficial**.
Unofficial reports say the president is about to resign.
The word is **unofficial**.

Spelling 1: The word is **eminent**.
Farida's aunt is an **eminent** physicist.
The word is **eminent**.

Spelling 2: The word is **bronchitis**.
Bronchitis typically causes a lot of coughing.
The word is **bronchitis**.

Spelling 3: The word is **rebellious**.
Feeling **rebellious**, Betty disobeyed her parents.
The word is **rebellious**.

Spelling 4: The word is **succumbed**.
Natasha **succumbed** to the temptation of a piece of cake.
The word is **succumbed**.

Spelling 5: The word is **marquis**.
The **Marquis** of Winchester is attending the event.
The word is **marquis**.

Spelling 6: The word is **league**.
Kit has been a member of our hockey **league** since 2004.
The word is **league**.

Spelling 7: The word is **dismissively**.
Hussein waved his hand **dismissively** at my objections.
The word is **dismissively**.

Spelling 8: The word is **insightfully**.
There was, Idris pointed out **insightfully**, another solution.
The word is **insightfully**.

Spelling 9: The word is **psychological**.
The police are building a **psychological** profile of the criminal.
The word is **psychological**.

Spelling 10: The word is **mettle**.
The team showed their true **mettle** during the last match.
The word is **mettle**.

Spelling 11: The word is **intertwined**.
The arch was adorned with **intertwined** carved figures.
The word is **intertwined**.

Spelling 12: The word is **thwart**.
The goblins made every effort to **thwart** the king's plans.
The word is **thwart**.

Spelling 13: The word is **laboratory**.
Dr Jekyll spent long days and nights in his **laboratory**.
The word is **laboratory**.

Spelling 14: The word is **imprudent**.
"Such action would be **imprudent**," Ameena warned.
The word is **imprudent**.

Spelling 15: The word is **transceivers**.
"What are **transceivers** used for?" asked Niall.
The word is **transceivers**.

Spelling 16: The word is **campaigned**.
Angie has **campaigned** against poverty for many years.
The word is **campaigned**.

Spelling 17: The word is **racquet**.
Taylor threw down his tennis **racquet** in a fit of anger.
The word is **racquet**.

Spelling 18: The word is **distraught**.
Learning he had lied to her, Juan's mother was **distraught**.
The word is **distraught**.

Spelling 19: The word is **re-energised**.
Serena felt **re-energised** after a relaxing weekend.
The word is **re-energised**.

Spelling 20: The word is **proficiency**.
Linda's **proficiency** in Japanese is truly remarkable.
The word is **proficiency**.

Spelling 1: The word is **psyche**.
The word **psyche** means the human mind, soul, or spirit.
The word is **psyche**.

Spelling 2: The word is **queue**.
Millie groaned as she saw the length of the **queue**.
The word is **queue**.

Spelling 3: The word is **archive**.
The librarian trawled through the **archive** to find the letter.
The word is **archive**.

Spelling 4: The word is **decaffeinated**.
I've started drinking **decaffeinated** tea.
The word is **decaffeinated**.

Spelling 5: The word is **whet**.
The knight began to **whet** the blunt blade of his dagger.
The word is **whet**.

Spelling 6: The word is **competition**.
Sayida has won this year's creative writing **competition**.
The word is **competition**.

Spelling 7: The word is **fiancée**.
Raja bought his **fiancée** a goldfish for her birthday.
The word is **fiancée**.

Spelling 8: The word is **beneficial**.
Computers can have a **beneficial** impact on children's learning.
The word is **beneficial**.

Spelling 9: The word is **anticlimax**.

After all the hype, the film itself was an **anticlimax**.
The word is **anticlimax**.

Spelling 10: The word is **pilfered**.
Kitty **pilfered** some sweets from the corner shop.
The word is **pilfered**.

Spelling 11: The word is **hindrance**.
Higher interest rates can be a **hindrance** to recovery.
The word is **hindrance**.

Spelling 12: The word is **complement**.
These pears make a nice **complement** to blue cheese.
The word is **complement**.

Spelling 13: The word is **rhythm**.
Rhythm is an important, if difficult, aspect of poetry.
The word is **rhythm**.

Spelling 14: The word is **phenomena**.
"These are recent **phenomena**," observed the anthropologist.
The word is **phenomena**.

Spelling 15: The word is **disastrous**.
The effects of global warming could be **disastrous**.
The word is **disastrous**.

Spelling 16: The word is **urgency**.
"I cannot stress the **urgency** of this enough," Lewis said.
The word is **urgency**.

Spelling 17: The word is **cryptically**.
"What is lost is found," said the soothsayer **cryptically**.
The word is **cryptically**.

Spelling 18: The word is **pronunciation**.
People's **pronunciation** will vary according to their dialect.
The word is **pronunciation**.

Spelling 19: The word is **transmission**.
The **transmission** of knowledge is becoming increasingly digital.
The word is **transmission**.

Spelling 20: The word is **irreconcilable**.
Irreconcilable artistic differences often cause bands to break up.
The word is **irreconcilable**.

TEST ADMINISTRATOR TRANSCRIPT 29

Spelling 1: The word is **inflammatory**.
Some protesters have been making **inflammatory** remarks.
The word is **inflammatory**.

Spelling 2: The word is **deducible**.
Is the date of this document **deducible** from its contents?
The word is **deducible**.

Spelling 3: The word is **mislabelled**.
The products were recalled as they had been **mislabelled**.
The word is **mislabelled**.

Spelling 4: The word is **pretentious**.
No one can stand Carl; he's so **pretentious**!
The word is **pretentious**.

Spelling 5: The word is **picturesque**.
The visitors were enchanted by the **picturesque** French village.
The word is **picturesque**.

Spelling 6: The word is **fluorescent**.
The **fluorescent** light bulb flickered as it came on.
The word is **fluorescent**.

Spelling 7: The word is **brigadier**.
Brigadier Sam Riley is hoping for a promotion.
The word is **brigadier**.

Spelling 8: The word is **hierarchy**.
Some animals have a complex social **hierarchy**.
The word is **hierarchy**.

Spelling 9: The word is **sequential**.
The word **sequential** means following a logical order.
The word is **sequential**.

Spelling 10: The word is **illegitimate**.
The opposition claimed the election was **illegitimate**.
The word is **illegitimate**.

Spelling 11: The word is **demoted**.
Our football club was **demoted** at the end of last season.
The word is **demoted**.

Spelling 12: The word is **begrudgingly**.
"Okay," Kyle said **begrudgingly** to his sister. "You're right."
The word is **begrudgingly**.

Spelling 13: The word is **inefficient**.
"This is a very **inefficient** way of doing things," said Fred.
The word is **inefficient**.

Spelling 14: The word is **atrocious**.
"My hair looks **atrocious**!" complained Elizabeth.
The word is **atrocious**.

Spelling 15: The word is **optician**.
On Tuesday, Ralph is going to see his **optician**.
The word is **optician**.

Spelling 16: The word is **disagreeable**.
"Mrs Bentu is extremely **disagreeable**," noted Viv.
The word is **disagreeable**.

Spelling 17: The word is **eiderdown**.
Arwa pulled the **eiderdown** over her head and went to sleep.

The word is **eiderdown**.

Spelling 18: The word is **alms**.
The kind-hearted prince gave **alms** to the poor.
The word is **alms**.

Spelling 19: The word is **referendum**.
Scotland recently held an independence **referendum**.
The word is **referendum**.

Spelling 20: The word is **glacial**.
The Ice Queen's beauty had a distinctly **glacial** quality.
The word is **glacial**.

TEST ADMINISTRATOR TRANSCRIPT 30

Spelling 1: The word is **nuclei**.
Most atomic **nuclei** consist of neutrons and protons.
The word is **nuclei**.

Spelling 2: The word is **sallow**.
The illness left him with an unhealthy, **sallow** complexion.
The word is **sallow**.

Spelling 3: The word is **aural**.
If something is **aural**, it is related to the sense of hearing.
The word is **aural**.

Spelling 4: The word is **hypocritical**.
It would be **hypocritical** of me to say I regret it; I don't.
The word is **hypocritical**.

Spelling 5: The word is **susceptibility**.
Some people's **susceptibility** to the flu is higher than others.
The word is **susceptibility**.

Spelling 6: The word is **voracious**.
Despite her **voracious** appetite, Pamela is very skinny.
The word is **voracious**.

Spelling 7: The word is **ineligible**.
People aged under 30 are **ineligible** for this offer.
The word is **ineligible**.

Spelling 8: The word is **eloquence**.
We were all taken aback by Shady's **eloquence**.
The word is **eloquence**.

Spelling 9: The word is **poltergeists**.
Ghosts that are noisy are called **poltergeists**.
The word is **poltergeists**.

Spelling 10: The word is **wrung**.
Lucy **wrung** the wet towel out in the sink.
The word is **wrung**.

Spelling 11: The word is **statistician**.
Otto works as a **statistician** at an investment company.
The word is **statistician**.

Spelling 12: The word is **rhetoric**.
The MP's speech was dismissed as empty **rhetoric**.
The word is **rhetoric**.

Spelling 13: The word is **complementary**.
The sum of two **complementary** angles is 90 degrees.
The word is **complementary**.

Spelling 14: The word is **malevolent**.
Pierre shivered at the demon's fierce, **malevolent** stare.
The word is **malevolent**.

Spelling 15: The word is **squawked**.
"Oooh! You scared me!" **squawked** Miranda.
The word is **squawked**.

Spelling 16: The word is **recipient**.
Who was the **recipient** of last year's Man Booker Prize?
The word is **recipient**.

Spelling 17: The word is **impertinence**.
Lady Earlham gasped at her daughter's **impertinence**.
The word is **impertinence**.

Spelling 18: The word is **extraterrestrial**.
The search for **extraterrestrial** lifeforms goes on.
The word is **extraterrestrial**.

Spelling 19: The word is **discourteous**.
It would be **discourteous** of us not to visit our friends.
The word is **discourteous**.

Spelling 20: The word is **machetes**.
Machetes are heavy, broad knives.
The word is **machetes**.

SPELLING LISTS

In the following lists, the government's 100 statutory words for Years 5 & 6 are indicated by an asterisk (e.g. category*).

TEST 1	TEST 2	TEST 3	TEST 4	TEST 5
category*	treasure	council	parliament*	harshly
recognised*	Who's	story	disapproval	precious
individual*	critic*	waltz	acknowledge	interview
Micro-organisms	lamb	delightful	awkward*	reliable
environment*	magically	grammar	impatient	favourite
alter	special	mishandled	stomach*	Temporary
bruise*	doubt	gnome	restaurant*	informal
illogical	Wednesday	literally	bough	orchestra
language*	profit	international	committee*	enviable
engineer	allowed	lessen	decision	fought
suggest*	misbehaved	invisible	variety*	quarter
definite*	Except	bizarre	quarts	biscuit
babysitter	cautious	chorus	explanation*	impolite
injustice	cereal	Deselect	attached*	chef
familiar*	charity	peel	flimsy	lead
repetitious	tough	impossibly	interfere*	thumb
deceived	height	anchovies	heroine	accident
accommodate*	disgrace	glamorous	sacrifice*	it's
democratically	preventable	course	delicious	cheerily
muscle*	incorrect	beige	According*	reaction

TEST 6	TEST 7	TEST 8	TEST 9	TEST 10
diligent	physical*	catalogue	guilt	conscious*
Scholars	aggressive*	occasion	import	empress
borders	wary	throat	outrageous	recipe
freight	desperate*	juiciest	ewe	harass*
substances	electrician	artificial	beliefs	frantically
alleys	twelfth*	conclusion	clockwise	shoulder*
strumming	handkerchiefs	menu	hangers	equipment*
invalid	cemetery*	breathe	misspellings	overpopulated
laps	election	indefinitely	subheading	occupy*
guidance	business	discouraged	lava	unimaginable
desert	achieve*	seized	extraordinary	forty*
hale	leisure*	coloured	semicircle	horde
unsatisfied	government*	misheard	unbearable	profession*
loan	chauffeur	they're	wear	misremembered
jealous	especially*	immediate*	pollution	appreciate*
library	conference	cyclist	fiasco	queasy
discarded	necessary*	Regrettably	hoard	system*
mistletoe	tomorrow	fabulous	loaves	correspond*
their	irresistible	cookies	characters	residential
sty	criticise*	irrational	Reindeer	identity*

SPELLING LISTS

TEST 11

adorable
mountainous
intersect
cough
eighth
where
conquered
isle
vicious
fragrance
swallowed
century
further
echoing
prophecy
information
disappear
improvement
Cheques
devised

TEST 12

peal
tolerance
inclined
microscopic
Inequality
duel
intermission
allies
tangibly
machinery
bicycles
pyre
disruptions
Fates
miscalculated
trough
packed
superstitious
sceptre
lone

TEST 13

excellent*
schemes
relevant*
bazaar
secretary*
available*
volcanoes
divisible
marvellous*
improbable
bachelor
foreign*
license
persuade*
martyr
communicate*
suspicious
crescent
interrupt*
rhyme*

TEST 14

sincere*
naively
confidential
piercing
misshapen
collaborate
applicable
irreversible
hygiene
moustache
strength
foe
bridle
nutritious
that's
disobedient
Although
extremely
scenery
measurements

TEST 15

admissible
mode
distilleries
gymnasium
chandeliers
advertisement
Quartz
diagrams
re-enactments
disturbance
counsel
reference
scissors
insistence
torpedoes
droughts
infamous
repelled
hail
disenchanted

TEST 16

bargain*
thorough*
signature*
route
convenience*
illiterate
lightning*
rhinoceroses
amateur*
offering
embarrass*
reincarnation
programme*
neighbour*
cologne
determined*
herbivorous
sufficient*
immediately*
disqualified

TEST 17

medicinal
resistant
ambitious
substandard
coincidence
architect
typical
reigns
Currants
superficial
completely
equipped*
dependent
brochures
disappointed
collectible
straight
rogue
conceive
anxiety

TEST 18

hazardous
viable
heiress
dissimilarity
reassured
boarders
submerged
transferred
Dual
clinician
syndicate
gilt
crises
Hypnosis
galaxies
tolled
dough
charismatic
commando
inaudible

TEST 19

soldier*
mistreatment
curiosity*
naval
vegetable*
submission
frequently*
wreck
conscience*
solemnly
exaggerate*
banquet
recommend*
average*
expectancy
occur*
conceited
develop*
crucial
prejudice*

TEST 20

readily
financial
automobile
address
fireman's
species
thistle
centre
ascent
disadvantages
accessible
impartial
education
platypus
calendar
series
typhoon
inhumane
adventurous
principal

SPELLING LISTS

TEST 21

offspring
coarse
synonymous
diagnosis
hoax
taut
complimentary
omissions
mowed
parachuted
Asymmetrical
woefully
larva
chiselled
imprecise
Oral
patriotism
irretrievable
luscious
storey

TEST 22

mischievous*
irregularity
accompany*
anniversary
symbol*
noticeably
existence*
troupe
sincerely*
gyroscope
inedible
dictionary*
unemployment
ancient*
foreword
ought
privilege*
autobiographical
community*
yacht*

TEST 23

chameleon
lenient
Dishonesty
hideous
antiques
separate
immigrated
borough
reimburse
antibiotics
substantial
Ordinarily
extension
bellowed
yield
misconduct
allegory
momentarily
symptom
commercials

TEST 24

prologue
sought
fungi
implausible
lapse
Inanimate
precarious
irreplaceable
eroded
widower
preceded
mythological
autonomous
fete (or fête)
unfashionable
isosceles
regeneration
pact
hysterically
colleagues

TEST 25

inadequate
temperature*
surveillance
guarantee*
miniature
opportunity*
technological
counterfeit
apparent*
imminent
sovereign
hangars
treacherous
nuisance*
martial
vehicle*
suite
negligence
controversy*
photosynthesis

TEST 26

mourning
responsibility
suspension
hoarsely
re-evaluated
tympani
Collapsible
fictitious
anarchy
parallel
impression
humongous
plagued
besieged
mosquitoes
anonymous
borne
pressure
shepherdess
Unofficial

TEST 27

eminent
Bronchitis
rebellious
succumbed
Marquis
league
dismissively
insightfully
psychological
mettle
intertwined
thwart
laboratory
imprudent
transceivers
campaigned
racquet
distraught
re-energised
proficiency

TEST 28

psyche
queue*
archive
decaffeinated
whet
competition*
fiancée
beneficial
anticlimax
pilfered
hindrance*
complement
Rhythm*
phenomena
disastrous*
urgency
cryptically
pronunciation*
transmission
Irreconcilable

TEST 29

inflammatory
deducible
mislabelled
pretentious
picturesque
fluorescent
Brigadier
hierarchy
sequential
illegitimate
demoted
begrudgingly
inefficient
atrocious
optician
disagreeable
eiderdown
alms
referendum
glacial

TEST 30

nuclei
sallow
aural
hypocritical
susceptibility
voracious
ineligible
eloquence
poltergeists
wrung
statistician
rhetoric
complementary
malevolent
squawked
recipient
impertinence
extraterrestrial
discourteous
Machetes

Printed in Great Britain
by Amazon